OUR LADY OF HOPE

OUR LADY OF HOPE

THE SOUL OF THE CATHEDRAL OF NOTRE DAME

PATRICK CHAUVET
RECTOR OF NOTRE DAME CATHEDRAL, PARIS

Paulist Press
New York / Mahwah, NJ

Cover image by anyaivanova/Shutterstock.com
Cover and book design by Lynn Else

Originally published as *Notre Dame d'Esperance*, Patrick Chauvet, copyright © 2019 by Presses de la Renaissance, Paris, France

Library of Congress Cataloging-in-Publication Data
Names: Chauvet, Patrick, author.
Title: Our lady of hope : the soul of the cathedral of Notre Dame / Patrick Chauvet.
Other titles: Notre Dame d'Esperance. English
Description: New York / Mahwah : Paulist Press, 2021. | "Originally published as *Notre Dame d'Esperance*, copyright 2019 by Presses de la Renaissance." | Summary: "Rector archpriest of Notre-Dame-de-Paris since 2016, Monseigneur Patrick Chauvet recounts the rhythm of his days. In charge of a world-famous basilica frequented by millions of visitors a year, historical monument, and above all a place of worship, he also gives us his vision of the Church today and the one he envisions for tomorrow"— Provided by publisher.
Identifiers: LCCN 2020018786 (print) | LCCN 2020018787 (ebook) | ISBN 9780809155118 (paperback) | ISBN 9781587689109 (ebook)
Subjects: LCSH: Notre-Dame de Paris (Cathedral) | Chauvet, Patrick. | Catholic Church—France—Paris—Clergy—Biography.
Classification: LCC BX4629.P3 N624713 2021 (print) | LCC BX4629.P3 (ebook) | DDC 282/.44361—dc23
LC record available at https://lccn.loc.gov/2020018786
LC ebook record available at https://lccn.loc.gov/2020018787

ISBN 978-0-8091-5511-8 (paperback)
ISBN 978-1-58768-910-9 (e-book)

Published by Paulist Press
997 Macarthur Boulevard
Mahwah, New Jersey 07430
www.paulistpress.com

Printed and bound in the
United States of America

To the Archbishop of Paris, the chaplains of the Cathedral, and its employees and volunteers: all my gratitude.

CONTENTS

Foreword ix
Caroline Pigozzi

Introduction 1

PART ONE: The Rector's Pastoral Mission

Chapter 1: The Mystery of Notre Dame 9

Chapter 2: Our Lady's Open Arms 20

Chapter 3: Home of the Sacred Crown of Thorns 31

Chapter 4: The Conversion of Paul Claudel 40

Chapter 5: Notre Dame, Mother and Teacher 50

Chapter 6: Notre Dame and Its Choir 61

Chapter 7: Preaching and Teaching at Notre Dame 71

PART TWO: Like Running a Small Business

Chapter 8: Being "the Boss" of a Small Business 79

Chapter 9: Victor Hugo's Notre Dame 89

Chapter 10: Fundraising 96

Chapter 11: Our Distinguished Guests 108

Chapter 12: The Adventure of Sound and Light: *Dame de Coeur* 118

PART THREE: The Future of the Cathedral

Chapter 13: Evangelization at Notre Dame 127

Chapter 14: Our Methods of Evangelization 136

Chapter 15: The Priorities of Mission 144

Chapter 16: A Priest First 154

Notes 175

FOREWORD

A FEW YEARS AGO, at a meeting of the board of directors of Radio Notre Dame, I was intrigued by the small nameplate of the person sitting beside me in a Roman collar: "Monsignor Patrick Chauvet." While one of the other members was digging for some numbers, I quietly asked him what he did. "Rector and archpriest of Notre Dame Cathedral," he replied a bit laconically, with a smile. The answer caught my interest, since I'd been living for several years on Paris's Île de la Cité, just in front of the Cathedral. On summer evenings, when the windows were opened, I could often hear the music of its great organ ascend to the sky.

At the end of the meeting, I was unable to resist asking my new acquaintance a long list of questions about his remarkable "job," and we made an appointment to talk further. He said he'd begun the pastoral assignment in September 2016, and he characterized the role as one of maintaining the feel of the place and the beauty of the liturgy. That's fine, but for an insatiably curious journalist and writer like me, it was not enough! So he elaborated for me, with patience and enthusiasm. It was then that I knew the experiences of this former literature teacher turned priest should not remain a secret. He had to share some of his rich experiences in a book. After all, Notre Dame, the most visited monument in France—before even the Louvre and the Eiffel Tower—had just celebrated its 850th anniversary!

Patrick Chauvet is the guardian angel of this church so steeped in history, with its 10 priests, 5 organists, and the 160 singers in its famous choir. He shares the great celebrations and solemn Masses of this landmark of spirituality, with its two majestic towers, with the archbishop of Paris, Michel Aupetit. It is the dazzling Cathedral where General de Gaulle notably sang the *Te Deum* under its celestial vaults on August 26, 1944, following the liberation of Paris from the Nazis; where, under the Fifth Republic, the funeral Masses of some of France's greatest figures have taken place; and where, more recently, massive crowds have gathered to pray for the victims of terrorist attacks.

Only a few years into his tenure, Msgr. Chauvet has already welcomed personalities such as Brigitte Macron, Melania Trump, the King and Queen of Sweden, former French President Valéry Giscard d'Estaing, the Supreme Allied Commander of Europe, and the President of the International Islamist League—in each case talking with them about God, sacred art, and the mysteries of Notre Dame Cathedral; to admire its three rose windows, those masterpieces of thirteenth-century Christianity, as well as the gargoyles and spiral staircases that are described so unforgettably by Victor Hugo in his historic novel that takes place there; and never forgetting the crypt or the chapel that houses treasures such as the very Crown of Thorns of Christ himself. It is a church that has received three popes—Pius VII, for the consecration and coronation of Napoleon I in December 1804; John Paul II, who celebrated Mass there in August 1997; and Benedict XVI, who led Vespers in September 2008.

Patrick Chauvet essentially runs a small business of sixty-seven employees and forty volunteers. This demands a lot of know-how, for here, even the Lord is a unionist! With thirty thousand visitors a day, in addition to all of the daily religious concerns, Msgr. Chauvet must manage the operating budget, the reception of visitors, the lighting, the heating, confessions, processions, the gift shop, the website, and even visits from police dogs sniffing for explosives prior to the arrival of important figures.

So how does he do it all? The serenity, the experience, and the humor of this priest—who was, between 1995 and 1999, rector of Paris's famous Sacred Heart Basilica—are almost miraculous. You'll learn about all of it in this book.

Notre Dame Cathedral is not just a parish but the pride of France—an imposing and fascinating monument that is even the site of three beehives from which Msgr. Chauvet makes honey! For the greater glory of God, of the people of Paris, and of tourists from all over the world.

Caroline Pigozzi
Author and *Paris Match* Senior Reporter

INTRODUCTION

ON THE DAY BEFORE Pentecost Sunday 2016, at around 11:00 a.m., the phone rang. I was in my office across the street from St. Francis Xavier Church, on Paris's Boulevard des Invalides, where I was pastor. I'd just had surgery on my right shoulder a few days earlier, and I was reading and looking out the window at the church that I loved so much.

It was the vicar general. He told me, "My dear Monsignor, I am calling to tell you that the cardinal-archbishop of Paris has just appointed you rector-archpriest of his Cathedral. Do you accept, even though you still have a year to go at St. Francis Xavier?"

Without hesitation I said yes because obedience to the bishop is a source of freedom. The auxiliary bishop had mentioned this possibility to me a few months earlier, but I was bound to silence about it.

After hanging up, I sat alone in my apartment. It was the end of eight years of happiness at St. Francis Xavier, a beautiful time of grace. But I was also hit by a whirlwind. How would I announce this appointment? It meant another move, and when a priest is also a professor of theology, there are some books in his library. But I did not rush to the Cathedral, where I was ordained on June 28, 1980, by a previous archbishop of Paris, Cardinal Marty.

As a canon and even dean of the chapter, I knew this spiritual landmark well, but not every nook and cranny, and I had not opened the closets, maybe for fear of running into Quasimodo!

Before entering the seminary at the Catholic Institute of Paris, I was a professor of classics at Sainte-Croix de Neuilly, a high school and college institution where I had once been a student myself. Teaching there was two years of joy. But it was a long time ago. Almost fifty years ago it was easy to teach about Racine, Pascal, Baudelaire, and so many others. (We will have the opportunity to discuss this later in this book.) Passionate about theater, I sometimes went on stage, and I even considered making it a career. But the Lord had other plans!

Seminary is a time of surrender; it is up to the church to confirm the call that a man thinks he hears. It is a time of spiritual struggle, where we consider carefully what we're choosing to give up. But being a seminarian isn't a vocation, and finally ordination arrived. At that point I was assigned to be chaplain at Sainte-Croix de Neuilly. First a student there, then teacher, then chaplain. I knew the place well; it has fostered many vocations. I met many happy priests there as a young man and a teacher, true educators in freedom who did not confuse teaching with discipline. And I must mention the boys' choir. I was alto, then tenor. It's a beautiful school of liturgy, community life, and self-mastery as well as a hotbed of vocations. My spiritual director had suggested that I pursue higher studies at Université Paris Nanterre. I studied classical literature and the students were smart and hardworking. This did not prevent me from participating in the life of the institution and getting involved in political activities.

I was chaplain at Sainte-Croix for three years and spent a lot of time thinking about the education of youth. This period had a big impact on me and has helped me in many ways in my ministry. Before ordination, the Archbishop of Paris had told us, "There will be a need for formation faculty in seminaries." In my prayer, I said to the Lord, "Anything but that!" Here again, the

Lord decides for us; but is not this the essence of the apostolic life? The apostles did not choose their mission; they received it.

After my first three years of ministry, I was appointed seminary director and professor of theology at the graduate level. This time, my summer was spent in the books! I had begun doctoral research on St. Basil, a Cappadocian father of the fourth century, which I completed during this period. I spent twelve years in the ministry of priestly formation. This too was a time of great grace. It's easy to see God working in the lives of young men who are preparing for the priesthood.

After six years at the Seminary of Saint-Sulpice, where I learned the trade, I moved to the Seminary of Paris and the Cathedral School, where I established the *studium*—the philosophical, theological, and exegetical program of studies—under the leadership of Cardinal Lustiger. During the summers, the seminarians and faculty did evangelization at the beaches of Brittany. So many memories!

Then it was time for a change. The cardinal appointed me rector of Paris's famous Sacred Heart Basilica—Sacré-Cœur. My mission was to renew pastoral care there, with the help of the Benedictine Sisters of the Sacred Heart. No small mission! There, too, it was necessary to manage the lay staff, tourists, and spiritual program. I discovered that I like challenges! And throughout those four years, I also discovered the spirituality of the Heart of Christ.

Then, too quickly, I was assigned to be director of the Office of Catholic Education in Paris and at the same time the headmaster of Saint-Jean de Passy, an elementary school and high school in the city. I was back in the world of education! It was three years of happiness, where I rediscovered my charism as teacher and spiritual father.

But then the cardinal assigned me to be the parish priest of Saint-Honoré-d'Eylau Church. Finally, parish ministry! I had begun to tell myself, "The Lord does not want to entrust you with a parish." Yet I had a deep desire for it in my heart. I was sad to leave Saint-Jean, but joyful at finally being called to parish ministry. But here again, the Lord leads us—I had not been in this assignment for very long when the archbishop invited me to dinner on a Sunday evening to announce that he was naming me vicar general. I thought the ceiling of the dining room had fallen on my head. He asked me to give up my commitments and to be available for this new mission. The move was not as hard this time because I hadn't even unpacked my books from their boxes.

I spent five years as vicar general, two with Cardinal Lustiger and three with Cardinal Vingt-Trois. A difficult mission! Accompanying priests, extinguishing fires, lighting others; the confirmations where I encountered the young people; the many pastoral visits that allowed me to discover the east side of Paris, the vitality of the parishes, and the wonderful work of the priests. Alongside this, there was the administration of the diocese and the assignments of priests. I learned quickly that these are not simple jobs. It was five years of discoveries and grace.

And then the man who was pastor of St. Francis Xavier Church was named a bishop and the parish needed a new pastor. The cardinal sent me there; he knew that I wanted to be a pastor and, to thank me for having accepted the role as his vicar general, he appointed me to this parish, with the additional tasks of preparing for Pope Benedict XVI's apostolic visit to Paris and also of managing the implementation in the archdiocese of Benedict's *motu proprio* on the Tridentine Mass. I accepted happily.

I was at St. Francis Xavier for eight years—years full of meetings, missions, and events! I could write a whole book about all that I experienced with the priests and parishioners there. I threw myself completely into that ministry, maybe to make up for those years when I had so desired to be a parish priest! I ate the entire apple, and this fruit was not forbidden!

Recently a young child, who had been watching the Vespers and spiritual programs from Notre Dame on our Catholic television station, KTO, asked me via the internet, "How does a person become the rector of Notre Dame?" And I answered him, "You let yourself be led by the Spirit!" When I look at all these years, I see a golden thread. All these different ministries have prepared me for my current ministry—educator, spiritual director, professor of theology, singer and liturgist, administrator, closeness to the faithful, pastoral charity, love of the church and the priesthood.

To be sure, everything was not always perfect! Each priest has his shortcomings, and he lives with them. "Grace," St. Thomas Aquinas said, "does not destroy nature." Ordination changes a man "for the better," said St. Gregory of Nyssa, but he remains what he is, with his own story. Those who work with me know that all too well.

After this long detour, let's go back to my office at St. Francis Xavier, after that call from the vicar general about my new assignment. First, I had to remain quiet about it until the official announcement. But of course, my spirit began to be elsewhere—the Île de la Cité, that island in the Seine, in the middle of Paris, where Notre Dame stands.

I knew I was entering into a story that was already in motion and that it was now my job to discern how best to steer this great ship, to get to know its team of chaplains and sixty-seven lay employees.

I arrived at the Cathedral not long after the November 2015 terrorist attacks on Paris. Tourists had begun to avoid the city, and even the faithful thought twice before coming to the Cathedral. But tourism is important to the Cathedral's financial well-being, and fewer tourists brought some financial difficulties. At the end of the month, there are bills to pay. But we had to trust in the Lord even in this.

During the summer of 2016, I rested in Brittany, preparing to begin my new ministry, to both build on the work of my predecessors and meet the new expectations of the faithful. Then

I arrived at Notre Dame on the evening of August 15, the Feast of the Assumption of Mary and the patronal feast of this Cathedral. It is on that day each year that the archbishop of Paris, at the end of the Marian procession at the Cathedral, repeats King Louis XIII's act of consecration of France to Our Lady. I was fifteen days early; my appointment would not officially begin until September 1.

I entered the Cathedral by myself, silently. I prayed while gazing upon the Virgin of Paris, the statue I loved so much. She is the head of this house, so it's important to be on good terms with her here! Since my ordination, I have always been moved while looking upon her tender face. This was never more the case than on that evening, as I was about to become the rector of her Cathedral.

Part One

THE RECTOR'S PASTORAL MISSION

1

THE MYSTERY OF NOTRE DAME

I BEGAN MY TENURE at Notre Dame Cathedral on September 1, 2016. The members of the staff welcomed me warmly, but it was only natural that each of them wondered about what lay ahead. Change is difficult, and there must be a process of "taming," as we learn in *The Little Prince*. Was I the fox or the little prince? Probably both at the same time! My predecessor had been there thirteen years, and habits had been formed.

We had to give each other time. Each rector has his own gifts and shapes the life of the Cathedral in his own way. So I watched, I listened, and, like any "boss," I studied the financial accounts—"the sinews of war," as they say. My time as rector at Sacré-Coeur had prepared me for that.

Income was down, so expenses had to be reduced because I didn't have a press to print money. The staff cooperated by agreeing to forego salary increases. I'm no economist, but common sense tells me when we must reduce costs.

But the Cathedral is the archbishop's, and he entrusts to the rector the role of making sure it meets the needs of the archdiocese and remains the radiant monument that it is. That means the archbishop and the rector need to maintain a good working relationship. When the new archbishop of Paris began his tenure here in January 2018, we met at length so that he could share with me his pastoral vision. Thereafter we began meeting every Sunday evening, before the 6:30 Mass, to share our concerns but also to develop our friendship. The archbishop must feel at home here, and that makes the rector happy, too.

I gradually discovered the scope of the mission entrusted to me. In many ways, I was running a small business, one that has cultural, political, and diplomatic dimensions, but also, thank God, a pastoral dimension, which is closest to my heart.

So let's start there. The liturgy is the center of the Cathedral's spiritual life. This has always been enriched by the Cathedral's office of sacred music, its organists, and the preaching of its priests. It has been a great joy and a great gift for me to experience such beautiful liturgies.

When my assignment to Notre Dame was announced, the organists, music director, and choir director all probably rushed to examine my Wikipedia page. If so, they'd have seen that I like choral singing and great music, from Gregorian to Palestrina, including Bach, Vivaldi, Monteverdi, and many others. When I was a young choir member, I participated in the international congresses of the Pueri Cantores, where I met Canon Jehan Revert, the great liturgist and music director at Notre Dame for many years, so even then I had shared in this beautiful musical and liturgical tradition.

The first major liturgy we had to prepare upon my arrival was my own installation by the cardinal. There can be no improvisation at Notre Dame...except when playing the organ! It is hard to understand all that is involved in such preparation. We had to choose the texts of the liturgy, plan the movement around the sanctuary, identify reserved places for the guests of honor—the entire event, from the clergy's departure from the sacristy until its return at the end.

Then there is the work of the sacristans. There are five of

them as well, and they are passionate about their work. They had to prepare all the chasubles, albs for priests who forgot to bring their own, ciboria for communion, altar cloths, the archbishop's chalice. Every detail is important.

The florists refresh the flowers in the Cathedral every week. A luxury? No, because flowers foster prayer. They surround the famous statue of the Virgin of Paris; large bouquets are placed in the Blessed Sacrament chapel and the Crown of Thorns chapel; and there are bouquets at the base of the ambo and the foot of the great bronze crucifix.

We must also mention the people who work at our Catholic television channel, KTO, and at Radio Notre Dame. Broadcasting sound from this enormous structure is not an easy task. The director, throughout any celebration, must control the sound balance, close one microphone while opening another, avoid feedback, and so on. The liturgy director is there to help with such tasks as the celebration goes on.

There are the people who work in technical services to prepare the Cathedral for major events. They install additional chairs, check the electricity, prepare the square in front of the Cathedral, and, in the case of my installation, make sure to have the keys to the building ready on the red cushion that the cardinal will present to me near the conclusion of the Mass.

And we can't forget the office that prepares the liturgy booklet before sending it off to the printer. Meanwhile, several workers must manage the schedule, the invitations, the mail, and so on. And the communications director organizes the presence of the media.

Just a word about security: The rector is well protected, especially since the November 2015 terrorist attacks in Paris. But of course, it's not just about the rector. The Cathedral is well protected because the building symbolizes the history of France—the monarchy, the Empire, and the Republic. It is also a part of Christian history. That's why security personnel are at the doors of the Cathedral to search visitors, and another team is attentive to the behavior of tourists who sometimes forget that they are in a church and of the faithful whose sometimes-mystical impulses are not always easy to manage.

The Cathedral closes at 7:00 p.m., but the work goes on. The organ manager checks the condition of the great organ, with its eight thousand pipes, and matches it with that of the chancel so that they are in tune with each other. Heat, dust, and variations in temperature all call for the attention of a specialist who is available twenty-four hours a day.

As happens every Friday, the heads of the Cathedral's various services—the sacristy, the main office, technical services, communications, the gift shop, security, the supervisors, and the head of economic affairs—met to settle the final details of the installation ceremony.

At 5:00 on Sunday evening, everything seemed ready. The altar servers had been ready for hours to serve the archbishop. These twenty-five young students receive spiritual formation on the mystery of the liturgy. They are available and their commitment is a precious aspect of the life of the Cathedral. Indeed, they provide their help during every Sunday celebration, as well as diocesan events, major processions, and the Holy Week liturgies. One cannot improvise being a great altar server; one can only become great at this ministry through experience. They serve not only the archbishop, but also the faithful. Their prayerful presence enhances the Cathedral's spiritual life.

I stood at the central portal to welcome political leaders as they arrived: Rachida Dati, mayor of Paris's 7th district (where I grew up), who came as a friend wanting to be present as I began this new adventure; Bernadette Chirac; Bernard Debré and a few other members of the National Assembly; the police chief; the commissioner of the 4th district; Anne Hidalgo, the mayor of Paris; representatives of France's Ministry of Culture; Bertrand Delanoë, attaché to the Cathedral and former mayor of Paris;

the commander of the police department motorcycle division. The presence of all these figures reminded me, if it were necessary, of the political dimension of this ministry that was now entrusted to me.

The Cathedral was filled, and my heart was full of joy. The celebration unfolded flawlessly, and as it ended, an altar server carried to the cardinal the famous cushion on which rested the massive keys to the Cathedral's doors. He entrusted them to me, asking me to allow the Cathedral to be open as often as possible, echoing the words of Pope Francis: "To go forth, go forth! For me this is the kernel of evangelization. And going forth means going somewhere, that is, closeness."[1]

After the liturgy, we had a large reception on the square in front of the Cathedral, where I encountered parishioners from past assignments and met new collaborators. This included the Knights of the Holy Sepulchre, whose presence is related to the Holy Crown of Thorns, entrusted to Notre Dame after the French Revolution, when the building was merely a museum. The Knights are the guardians of this singularly unique relic, on which I will reflect later in this book.

The reception was like a whirlwind under the lights of this 850-year-old square! After the last guests left, I went to my room exhausted, and, after praying evening prayer, quickly plunged into the arms of Morpheus, with many dazzling images dancing in my head.

The rector gets up early because he goes to bed early. I have always had a well-regulated life, probably a little monastic, in fact. But the future belongs to people who get up early.

When the doors open, I enter the Cathedral. I sit before the statue of the Virgin of Paris. Calm reigns and ideas begin to come to life in my head. I reflect on my primary challenge—to help tourists become pilgrims—and another—to ensure that the faithful find what they are looking for. I often pray there in the morning or in evening after closing. These are moments of spiritual rest, when the silence is beautiful. Only the stones speak, and they tell the story of Notre Dame.

The priority of priorities is the spiritual life. It is the soul of the Cathedral. But how to serve the millions of visitors who are so far from our faith? So many do not understand what this place is about; they are amazed by the majesty of its architecture, but otherwise it means little to them. Some, with their cell phones in hand, complete a visit in just over three minutes, checking off one more spot on the tourist circuit. But it only takes a light breeze for God to intervene in someone's life. I need to work on the notion of "mystery."

We begin the day. I turn on the lights, and the chapels came back to life: the paintings are illuminated, the altars are prepared in white cloths, and some boxes that a worker had left on a dolly in a corner have disappeared. But where people seek God, the devil loves to prowl.

It doesn't take much for the mystery of Notre Dame to become for visitors a sacred mystery. Let me share with you some convictions. Every visitor, whether a tourist or one of the faithful, is by nature and vocation a religious being. As the *Catechism of the Catholic Church* says, "Coming from God, going toward God, man lives a fully human life only if he freely lives by his bond with God" (no. 44).[2] The square outside is a forum filled with the troubles of the world; as one enters the Cathedral, a little darker than the outside, one can almost hear Psalm 42 resonating:

> As a deer longs for flowing streams,
> so my soul longs for you, O God. (v. 1)

We are seekers of God, but let us not forget that God seeks us, too. Often, God is hidden behind a pillar of the Cathedral, in the sunlight that illuminates one of the three rose windows, in the voice of one of the soloists of the choir, in a passage of the word of God proclaimed from the ambo, or in the smile of a chaplain blessing a medal for a pilgrim—who can know?

In our world, where we live so superficially, we are drying out, cut off from the source of living water. The Cathedral offers a source of living water, but it is necessary to guide the faithful to the source, and this is the liturgy.

To cross the threshold of the dwelling place of God expresses a trust in God. That's why this building can never be just a museum. Every spiritual story is unique; at Notre Dame, we hope to awaken the desire that is in the depths of each person's heart. What images of God have we fashioned for ourselves? There is a trap: many don't want to see God, but merely give God a face; but God has no face (or rather, God has but one face, the one he took in the incarnation). The visitor must be willing to be surprised and forget his or her own images of God—the moralizing father, the bogeyman, the judge—otherwise, we miss the mystery! One doesn't simply visit Notre Dame—one goes in search of God. Some are afraid to enter this holy place because they feel unworthy; they find it hard to believe that God loves them after all they have done! But God is waiting for each of us as we are.

Happy is the person who, drawing close to God, will be able to say, "I have seen God!" It is a beautiful spiritual experience to perceive the light and to be touched by God's presence, for one's soul to recognize this light and each divine touch.

Unlike Buddhism, which understands the effort of arriving at Nirvana to be an entirely *human* effort, the Christian must be open to *grace*. The pastoral work of the rector is to try constantly to make sure that nothing prevents the work of grace. It takes so little for a person to close his or her heart like an oyster—an unpleasant greeting, an irritating remark, a harsh glance, a moralizing attitude. But one can also understand the challenges that the supervisors in the Cathedral face, trying to maintain a fitting silence, asking for proper dress, especially in summer! I made dress requirements in the Cathedral a bit more demanding, to remind visitors that being in the Cathedral is different than a visit to the beach. It's a matter of respect for the Lord and for the faithful who come there to pray. I've been criticized for this by tourists, who have called me a fundamentalist. I'm not. But I am attached to basic rules of politeness that help us live together. I've always thought that we should give etiquette courses, from elementary school through university!

Let's go back to the source of the mystery. But be careful—the word *mystery* can be ambiguous. We're not talking about something esoteric, like the Eleusinian mysteries or the prophecies of the Oracle of Delphi in ancient Greece. No, "the mystery" is the Father's loving plan, hidden for centuries and made manifest by the incarnation of the Son of God. As Cardinal Ratzinger (later Pope Benedict XVI) reminded us, "We must recover the dimension of the sacred in the liturgy....It is absolutely useless for the parish priest to bang his head to come up with who knows what idea or imaginative novelty.... The essential thing in the liturgy is the mystery."[3] And that is why participation in the liturgy is not primarily about *doing*, but about listening, being open, receiving. That was the disposition of the young Paul Claudel, who was touched by what was totally beyond him while at Christmas Vespers, standing next to the statue of the Virgin of Paris, in 1886.

We don't need a sumptuous liturgy for people to experience the mystery. A simple morning Mass in the Pietà chapel, with the rising sun coming through the stained-glass windows in shimmering colors that dapple the victorious cross and Mary holding the dead Christ in her arms, can lead us to the Invisible One.

Many tourists cannot access the chapel at the back of the sanctuary; they have other places to put themselves in the presence of God. But those who attend the 8:00 and 9:00 weekday morning Masses have this opportunity, as do some distinguished visitors or those who are led by one of the members of our association of volunteer guides, the Communauté d'Accueil dans les Sites Artistiques (CASA).

How can we not stop to think here about the great religious and political moments of history to which the Cathedral has been so intimately linked?

There are shining moments, like August 18, 1239, when King St. Louis, barefoot and dressed in the simple tunic of a penitent, came to deposit our Lord's Holy Crown of Thorns prior to it being moved to the sacred chapel where it would stay for centuries.

There are darker moments, like the coronation of Queen Isabeau of Bavaria, the wife of the "mad and beloved" King Charles VI, in 1389; or the same king's funeral in 1422, when the two bells of the Cathedral, "Marie" and "Jacqueline," sounded the knell of the French monarchy; or when the child-king, Henry VI of England, was crowned king of France by the bishop of Winchester in 1431.

There are happy moments of royal weddings: the marriage of Francis II, the Dauphin of France, to the young Queen of Scotland Mary Stuart in 1558; of King Henry of Navarre, the future Henry IV, to Marguerite de Valois ("Queen Margot") in 1572; and of the Emperor Napoleon III to Eugénie de Montijo in 1853. Or the nineteenth-century baptisms of the heir of the House of Bourbon, the Duke of Bordeaux; Prince Philippe of Orléans, Count of Paris; and the son of Emperor Napoleon III, the *prince impérial*.

The Cathedral vaults resounded again on March 10, 1687, with the voice of Bishop Bossuet preaching the funeral sermon of *le Grand Condé*, Louis II, which was said to be the greatest and most beautiful address ever spoken there.

The national role of the Cathedral of Notre Dame took further shape in April 1302, when King Philip IV the Fair convened the first meeting of the Estates General there. And it entered even more fully into the history of the nation at the time of the French Revolution, when it was established as the temple of a national "religion." The first great manifestation of this role was the coronation of Napoleon Bonaparte as Emperor of the French on December 2, 1804.

There were the *Te Deums* sung there to mark the military victories of November 1918 and May 1945; General de Gaulle coming to celebrate the liberation of Paris there in 1944, to the playing of Bach's *Magnificat*; but also the national funeral of President Carnot in 1894, in the midst of the conflict between the church and the Republic; and the twentieth-century celebrations of the funerals of Presidents de Gaulle, Pompidou, and Mitterrand—each of these moments have confirmed the special place that Notre Dame Cathedral has had in maintaining our national unity.

And, of course, how can we not recall Cardinal Pacelli (the future Pope Pius XII) evoking, in 1937, in unforgettable terms, the Christian vocation of the French nation, or the visits of St. John Paul II and Pope Benedict XVI during their pastoral visits to France in 1980 and 2008, respectively?

When the rector is alone in the Cathedral, sitting quietly in the darkness before the Pietà, he sometimes remembers these moments in history. I recall how on February 10, 1638, King Louis XIII, by a solemn consecration, placed the kingdom of France under the protection of the most holy and glorious Virgin Mary. The Cathedral preserves the perpetual memory of this act with the two statues of Kings Louis XIII and Louis XIV praying at the foot of the Pietà. This vow is renewed every year, on the Feast of the Assumption, at the time of the great Marian procession, a magnificent testimony to the history of our country.

And the beautiful pages of history that we "read" inside this Cathedral didn't stop turning with General de Gaulle. The more recent visits of St. John Paul II and Benedict XVI and the large gatherings of people following terrorist attacks all remind us of what an integral part of France this place still is today.

The rector is part of this story and he must, in whatever ways he is able, carry it on. There is sometimes a dizziness in anticipation of the chance to write a new page of this remarkable story. Notre Dame is the precious jewelry box that holds the treasures that have made France what it is. It is here that we write our story.

2

OUR LADY'S OPEN ARMS

DID YOU KNOW that Notre Dame Cathedral is one of the places in Paris where divine mercy flows for seven hours every day? Priests are always there to welcome pilgrims and tourists who wish to go to confession or just talk. Many of these priests speak several languages—English, Italian, Spanish, Japanese, German, Creole, Bandara, Lebanese Arabic, Fang, Lingala, Ukrainian, Portuguese, Catalan, Mossi, and more.

The Cathedral welcomes the entire world, but the rector has a disability—he speaks only French! Fortunately, many French speakers come to Notre Dame to take a step on their spiritual journey.

What extraordinary encounters! God works wonders. And the Virgin Mary is involved—she draws the faithful with tenderness. How many people, young and old, wonder how they ended up sitting there in front of a priest!

Mary calls from the square in front of the Cathedral, "Come, come, my Son wants to meet you."

"But I have nothing to say to him!"

"What does it matter? He wants to tell you, 'I love you!'"

Obviously, we won't reveal what is said in our two welcome centers. It's part of God's secret. But the welcome center is a privileged place of grace. It serves in a way like a store's display window, a first encounter for many pilgrims who have no other point of reference. Some have not entered a church for years. The chaplains of Notre Dame are there, smiling like the father who waited on his doorstep for the return of his prodigal son. Smiling, but mostly listening! I am always struck by the fact that in this world in which we're all so "connected," we don't seem to know how to communicate anymore. The screen is too often a shield or barrier.[1] Nothing is more beautiful than when the eyes of two people meet. But it evokes such fears—fear of the truth, even if it is a truth that liberates our hearts!

There is a spirituality of welcome; this is where the maternal dimension of the church lives. The face of Christ, the face of the church, the maternal face of welcome, and the face of the one who welcomes are superimposed. It is through these faces that the presence of the Lord is made known. We can never forget that when we welcome another person, we welcome the presence of the Lord. Such an encounter requires great qualities; it is a moment when one forgets oneself in order to take an interest in the other. Freely giving one's attention to another is a true gift of oneself. If the encounter is authentic, it enriches even the life of the one who welcomes, helping to bring cohesion to the scattered elements of her own life. These elements will acquire new life and meaning. So many people live such tormented, agitated lives in need of unity! As the Psalmist says, "Give me an undivided heart" (Ps 86:11). The conversations that we have can help a believer to come closer to herself, that is, to draw closer to Christ, to return to Christ's heart, the source of the unification of her own self.

When one person looks into the face of another, we become, in a way, companions. There is an exchange of hearts. To give life, to unveil, to participate in the redemption of the world that is none other than life given in abundance—that is one of the essential roles of welcoming.

Isn't another role to help someone welcome the Lord into his life? In a world that is so often dark, the priest can be a reflection of light that is a foretaste of the moment when everything will be light. The people who come to see us carry heavy burdens, and they seek, through these encounters, to lay them down. They take a step back, open their hearts, and allow the Lord to embrace them! This is not the work of a "shrink," but of a shepherd. We do it for free. The priest doesn't take the place of the psychoanalyst, of course; he can't because he's not trained for that. But his ministry is about opening new ways for grace to work in the life of the one who seeks counsel. Spiritual blindness is not uncommon—"God was there, and I didn't know it!" The priest must ask for the gift to understand hearts. It is not easy to treat a wound, and we are here to heal.

Offering this kind of welcome is part of the rector's work. And though it happens within certain office hours, it is not limited to that. My office is one place, but it also happens in the reception area, in the square, in the chapter room, in the sacristy, before the statue of the Virgin of Paris—so many times and places. I wish I could spend twenty-four hours a day doing this. But there are other tasks that need attention. But these encounters amaze me and nourish my life of faith. Most often, they are brief encounters that happen too fast, but what does it matter? The good Lord is at work. Unlike in a parish, where there is a chance for follow-up, in a pilgrimage site like ours, the faithful move on; for a rector who used to be a pastor, this brings a sense of loss. But we should not ignore someone's eye contact that expresses distress. It is not uncommon to be able to offer a word of hope to a person crushed by some pain, like the death of a loved one. If I don't speak that person's language, I have only the language of facial expressions and gestures; compassion can often be transmitted that way. On the day of my ordination to priesthood, my bishop anointed my hands with holy chrism. From then on, the Spirit passes through these hands. I often think about it when I am giving a blessing, extending my hands. Such proximity is a source of joy and trust.

The welcome of pilgrims is also a highlight. They come from all over the world. Chinese, Americans, Japanese, and Australians; Belgians, Italians, and Spaniards; and so many others. But why do they come to Notre Dame?

First, there is the beauty of the place; entering the Cathedral is magical. Anyone who takes the time to stop and look around can only be awestruck. It is so sad to see some tourists run through the place at the speed of racehorses. With their cameras in their hands, they photograph things they don't even look at, so that when they get home they can say, "We *did* Notre Dame!" But they didn't see anything!

Fortunately, many people take the time to sit down. And you cannot see everything at once; you must visit more than once to discover the various works of art. I remember, after we installed more lights in the chapels, a person familiar with the place said to me, "Father, you did well by lighting these paintings." They had been there a long time, but they were not easily seen.

I am convinced that beauty has a fundamental way of revealing God. Art is the transfiguration of reality, its relationship to the absolute. The artist paints the external form of things but reveals the mystery or the force that inhabits the form.

Artists are supposed to know the deep bitterness of the distance between the fire of their mind, the force of contemplation, and the realized work. But the theologian also suffers from this distance: we cannot contain God in our works of spirituality, and to that I say, Thank God! If we knew everything about God, there would be nothing left to desire of heaven!

Artists seek the transfiguration of matter. Christian artists seek to use their talents to make the Invisible visible. The French novelist André Malraux said that "the only place where the divine is visible is in art, whatever name it is given." The role of art is therefore essential because it allows us to touch the eternal. I like to recall the comment of Henri Matisse: "Do I believe in God? Yes, when I work. If I am open and humble, I feel the help of Someone who allows me to do things well beyond my abilities."

If Christian art were to fall into crisis, it would be a sign of the loss of what is eternal in humanity, and we would be in danger of losing something that pushes us toward eternity. The artist surrenders himself so that his work might reflect the eternal and in some way give glory to God. Christian art is charged with the presence of God.

The theologian Maurice Zundel said, "There are many works of art, but beauty is one. Each work expresses an aspect of beauty, but none exhausts it. All are immersed in the mystery and participate in its eternity. All works of art are beautiful; none is beauty itself."

It is necessary, of course, to distinguish aesthetic beauty from beauty in biblical terms. Everyone will have his or her own response to a work of art because beauty is subjective, like love and longing. The aesthetic experience is one of the joys of the soul. I never tire of looking at the fourteenth-century statue of the Virgin of Paris.

But must we limit ourselves to aesthetics? We must go beyond it to discover the tender maternity of Mary.

God said to Moses, "I will make all my goodness pass before you" (Exod 33:19). In the Hebrew, this word translated here as *goodness* refers to beauty, splendor, glory. Here is a key: divine beauty is one of the properties of being, a relationship of love; beauty foreshadows the mission of salvation entrusted to Christ by his Father. Through the Cathedral, we discover that beauty is part of the history of salvation. Beauty cannot be an individualistic search; its vocation is to remind us of our harmony with God, a harmony rooted in love. What is beautiful is good and true. And so, the mission of the artist is to reveal beauty because only then can truth be known and goodness reign. Before such beauty, humanity can be caught up in an eternal gaze, brought back to the connection between heaven and earth, reminded of the purpose of its own existence, caught up in a relationship of love revealed by beauty.

As rector, I am fortunate to have time to *stop* to contemplate a painting or a statue. I like to approach it, contemplating it in its sacred space, which teaches me about divine harmony and about our participation in this harmony. The empty Cathedral is a call to transcend myself. I might get nervous about getting locked inside, but I remind myself that I have the key and that the guards are nearby. And of course, there are the occasional mice that emerge in the evening, to take back their territory! I must admit that I'm afraid of these little animals, like the rats who come out at night into the square in front of the Cathedral to finish the sandwiches thrown in the bushes. It makes me hurry a bit when I'm heading out to my car.

When pilgrims come to the Cathedral, it is to encounter Mary, the Mother of Mercy. She reveals to us the true face of our God, which is a face of tenderness. It is a grace to contemplate this.

How often is the Hail Mary prayed by someone in tears? It is the prayer of a person who can no longer find their own words to cry out their misery and weakness!

Its opening words remind us of the mystery of love between God and humanity. Two faces—God and humanity—encounter each other, look at each other, recognize each other. Just as when we meet someone, we call her by her first name and then by the surname that identifies who she is, so we do in this prayer: "Hail Mary, full of grace." This latter is the source of her beauty, for grace flourishes in her. The Immaculate reminds us that grace is more original than sin. What hope this offers us who are such sinners!

Then we express who Mary is before God: "The Lord is with you." And we acknowledge that she is blessed by God; she lives unceasingly in the presence of God.

We remember the One she loves and who loves us: "Blessed is the fruit of your womb, Jesus." Mary wants to lead us to the source, to her Son, the redeemer of humanity, the only Savior. Mary never puts herself in the place of her Son—on the contrary! She leads us to the dwelling place of the Father and the Son.

And then comes our audacious request: "Pray for us sinners." We present ourselves to her—who is the blessed one of God, the pure source, the Immaculate—with our poverty, our weaknesses, our unruly tendencies. But we know that we're only talking to her about concerns that she already shares, like any mother. In completing this Hail Mary, we can ask her that because of our kinship, Christ might become for us what he was for her, a living person, preferred to everything, "now and at the hour of our death."

How can we not recall here the words of the Curé of Torcy in George Bernanos's great novel *The Diary of a Country Priest*?

> Yes, lad, to pray to her as you should you must feel those eyes of hers upon you: they are not indulgent... they are eyes of gentle pity, wondering sadness, and with something more in them, never yet known or expressed, something which makes her younger than sin, younger than the race from which she sprang, and though a mother, by grace, Mother of all grace, our little youngest sister.[2]

Mary attracts so many pilgrims and faithful because she brings mercy. She radiates the beauty of divine mercy that transforms everything, the beauty that divine mercy sends down upon the world.

From the Virgin of Paris statue, we can turn our gaze to the Pietà at the back of the sanctuary. This sculpture is the work of Nicolas Coustou, completed in 1723. He represented Mary at the foot of the cross, weeping over the corpse of her Son, expressing a mother's pain and her perfect submission to the will of God. We are at Golgotha, the summit of mercy. The whole tradition of the church locates the intercession of the Virgin here, at the foot of the cross, where Christ entrusts to her St. John, who represents each one of us. Jesus, saying to his Mother, "Behold your Son," asks her for an ultimate giving up of herself; she would have liked to be attentive to her suffering and dying Son on the cross, and now her Son asks her to take care of John and, with him, all the disciples. This is where we must situate Mary's participation in the mystery of mercy.

We mustn't think that Mary took the place of her Son; she is not independent of Jesus. All that we admire in her she has received from her Son. She is not a mediator between the Father and the Son; she is a mediator between Christ and us. This means that she leads us to the source of mercy. She is close to every sinner; it is our sin that prevents us from being close. Mary recognizes every human being as a sister or brother, whatever we have done, even if we are in the depths of despair, overwhelmed by our sin. She sees us as infinitely worthy of being loved; that's why I love her face of tenderness. Often, sitting before Our Lady, I read this meditation by the art historian Dominique Ponnau, a renowned admirer of our Cathedral:

> Our Lady of the Threshold is the one we humbly come here to pray to....We need only to gaze upon her. To

> entrust our needs to her. To rely on her for what we entrust to her care....Perhaps then, before her solemn beauty and that of her Son, we will each begin, or begin again, to cross from the Lady of the Threshold to the Lady of the Port, the ultimate port, whose eternal light will tear the night away.

Mary welcomes all people, with their history and their freedom. She bears each person in her hope; she does not exclude any of us because of preconceived ideas. What is the secret of Our Lady of Paris? She sees every person who enters "her home" as a beloved creature of God and called to freedom. Her happiness is to love us as we are. She loves the beauty of our hearts, even if there are shadows there. Her mercy is her discreet but effective accompaniment of each of us until the hour of our death. The light of mercy shines on Mary's face, which is why she is the most beautiful of all women.

What does one ask of Our Lady of Paris? I receive many prayer requests, thanks to our Catholic television station that broadcasts our Vespers service throughout France every evening. All these intentions are included in my intercessory prayer—requests for healing, for the suffering of loneliness that many old people experience, alone and abandoned. How could one not be moved by the words of an elderly person who is thankful for the fact that Jesus created her dog who, when she is crying, comforts her? Such pain reflected in a letter like this! Before we even cry out our distress, Mary, because she knows ours hearts, joins us and comforts us.

One day, a young man stopped me in the Cathedral and said to me, "Father, I have no more faith, and yet here I am. I didn't plan to come in here, but something pulled me inside." We were near the Virgin of Paris statue, so I pointed to her tender face and told the man, "Here's the one to blame." This young man began to cry; the Son did the rest to dry his tears.

Mary leads us to her Son. Many pilgrims find it difficult to meet her Son; Mary helps them because she knows that he wants to touch their wounds to heal them. And how does he heal them? By revealing the loving face of his Father.

At Lourdes, as at Notre Dame, we ask for the healing of hearts, the grace to accept our sinful past, to accept our weaknesses, to open our hearts so that her Son can heal our wounds.

We are still so marked by Jansenism. We must beware of becoming rigid moralists. The idea of divine justice is that God gives each person their due; God gives to everyone what they deserve, in a sort of distributive justice—he distributes rewards if we have done good and punishments if we have done wrong. But if that is all we are aware of, then we strive to do good because we're afraid of God. We forget that God's distributive justice and his salvific justice, the justice that saves us, are not opposed. On the contrary, they are related. In his relationship with us, God decides not to be limited to strict justice, but to save us freely and mercifully. Strict justice is not, for God, the last word.

Beyond strict justice, God is love and mercy. Love goes beyond justice. It does not eliminate justice but includes it. In God, justice and mercy are one. God is just by being faithful to what he is, which is merciful love.

We in the church have spoken too often about the punitive justice of God. Let's admit that we didn't do a great job of it. There is no vengeance in God, for if there is, then God is not love. God responds to evil and sin only through love. Like "little Thérèse," I often meditate on Christ's words to Nicodemus: "For God so loved the world that he gave his only Son, so that everyone who believes in him may not perish but may have eternal life" (John 3:16). If I refuse to believe, I put myself in a position to be judged. But by faith and love, the disciple has already passed from death to life. So as Thérèse asked, "What should I fear then?"[3] She wrote in her last letter that God "is but love and mercy."[4]

Some believers talk a lot about divine justice and the idea of offering oneself to divine justice. In my preaching, I propose offering ourselves to merciful love. Divine justice may be more reassuring to some, but to offer oneself each day to love is a spiritual adventure, and this is the true God. Mary our Mother encourages us to go to this source.

I sometimes meet Christians who have a terrible fear of the judgment of God. At those times I turn to "little Thérèse," who often accompanies me: "There is only one way to force the Good Lord not to judge us for everything, and that is to present ourselves to Him with empty hands....Don't hold anything back. Give your good deeds up to Him as soon as you do them." At the Cathedral, thanks to the tenderness of Our Lady, we, like Therese, can offer ourselves to love, because "for the sacrificial victims of love, it seems to me that there will be no judgment. Rather, the Good Lord will hurry to repay, with eternal delights, His own love that He will see burning in their hearts....*We are consumed by love only insomuch as we give ourselves over to love.*"[5]

These are not just pious words; it is the very message of the gospel: "...so that everyone who believes in him may not perish but may have eternal life." Faith, trust, abandonment do not excuse me from being good, but they allow me to know the tenderness of God, because this tenderness has been poured upon me.

This is the pastoral program that is based on the liturgy and seeks to emphasize merciful love through the presence of Mary, the Virgin of tenderness. When we fix our eyes on her face, her smile appears; it takes time, but it is a beautiful experience.

3

HOME OF THE SACRED CROWN OF THORNS

I AM SURE THAT even many French people don't know that the Sacred Crown of Thorns is at Notre Dame Cathedral. And yet, after the Shroud of Turin, it is the most important relic of Christendom.

Let's start with a bit of history, without going into too much detail.

We find reference to the Crown of Thorns in the writings of St. Paulinus of Nola in AD 409. The saint mentions that it is among the relics at a basilica on Mount Zion in Jerusalem. But why are there nearly four centuries between the crucifixion of Jesus and the first evidence of the existence of this relic? This is simply because in the first centuries, Christians kept the relics, but did not venerate them.

Due to the threat of invasion by the Persians, the Crown was transferred to Constantinople shortly before 614. In the eleventh and twelfth centuries, many Western and Eastern pilgrims went there to venerate this precious relic.

In 1204, during the fourth crusade, the city of Constantinople was sacked, but the Church of the Virgin of the Pharos, which the Crusaders called "the Holy Chapel," was spared because many sacred relics were present there, the Crown among them. The Latin emperors of the Byzantine Empire, facing financial problems, sold many of these relics. In 1238, the Latin emperor Baldwin II, in need of financial support, offered the Crown of Thorns to King Louis !X (who would later be canonized a saint). The king decided to acquire it—and paid a cost that represented, at the time, half of the annual budget of the kingdom!

The Crown arrived on August 10, 1239, at Villeneuve-l'Archevêque, in north-central France, where it was welcomed by the holy king himself and then transported by him to Notre Dame Cathedral. Walking barefoot as an expression of humility, Louis IX presented it there in a solemn celebration. From there, it was brought to the royal chapel of the king's residence, the Palais de la Cité, in the center of Paris, until the completion in 1248 of the Sainte-Chapelle, a stunning chapel within the Palais de la Cité built to house the relics.

In March 1791, to protect the Crown amid the mayhem of the French Revolution, King Louis XVI moved it to the Abbey of St. Denis, north of Paris. But two years later, during the Reign of Terror, the treasure was deposited in the Cabinet des Médailles, a museum of the National Library of France. A miracle? It surely was, because during this tumultuous time, it would have taken little for the Crown to be discarded or destroyed!

On October 28, 1804, the precious relics were transferred to the Cathedral. In 1923, Cardinal Louis-Ernest Dubois, the archbishop of Paris, entrusted to the Knights of the Holy Sepulcher the role of serving as guardians of the Sacred Crown.

I am often asked, "Is this the *true* Crown of Thorns?" I point out that in all the world, no other cathedral or church claims to have such a relic. Only Notre Dame has this grace. I also say that I am constantly struck by the spiritual radiance that touches those who venerate it. The Crown touches hearts and souls. Tourists who are present when it is displayed for veneration do not always understand what is happening, but they are struck by the great silence that pervades the Cathedral, reflecting the peace in the hearts of those present.

In September 2008, Pope Benedict XVI venerated the Crown during his apostolic visit to Paris. On that occasion, at a celebration of Vespers following his veneration of the relic, the pope said to the congregation gathered there, "Notre Dame Cathedral rightly remains one of the most celebrated monuments of your country's heritage. Following a tradition dating back to the time of Saint Louis, I have just venerated the relics of the True Cross and the Crown of Thorns, which have now found a worthy home here, a true offering of the human spirit to the power of creative Love."[1]

Powerful people who come to the Cathedral, especially those who are faithful, often request an opportunity to venerate the Crown privately. For them, the Crown is an icon that exudes a divine energy, that of salvation.

I know the Moscow Patriarchate would like to have the Crown for three days, but it cannot leave Notre Dame. There are certainly some exceptions—such as a procession to the Holy Chapel that took place on the occasion of the 850th anniversary of the Cathedral—but it cannot leave the grounds. So Russian dignitaries make the pilgrimage. Generally, I receive them after the church closes, at about 7:15 p.m. A choir of Orthodox seminarians sings litanies; I wait at the Saint-Étienne portal to welcome the clergy, the ambassadors, and their wives. We go together to the chapel where the relic is, and the choir begins to sing. We read a passage from Scripture that refers to what we are going to live spiritually: "Then the soldiers of the governor took Jesus into the governor's headquarters, and they gathered the whole cohort around him. They stripped him and put a scarlet robe on him, and after twisting some thorns into a crown, they put it on his head" (Matt 27:27–29). This mockery is prophetic; it proclaims that Christ is indeed the king of the universe, but not in the manner of temporal kings.

We then open the chest, remove the Crown, and set it on the cushion. We sit in silence. With our eyes closed, we are in Jerusalem. Images of the crowned Christ parade before our eyes. Salvation is real. All this explains the emotion and the tears of so many of the faithful who experience this moment. Those present have encountered the Suffering Servant. Venerating the Crown, like praying before a crucifix, reminds each of us of our own sins.

I like to tell the following parable, which is not found in any of the four Gospels. A Martian arrives on Earth and visits churches. He is surprised to see crosses and questions two Christians in prayer, "What is this cross?" The first answers, "Oh, it's an old story. Almost two thousand years ago, Jesus was crucified because he called himself Son of God. The fact is, he came too early, because if he had become incarnate among us today, we would certainly never have crucified him!" But the second Christian replies, "That's not so. If Christ came today, the crucifixion would happen all over again." And the Martian concludes, "You people are monsters." Yes, we are monsters, and that's why Christ came into the world! He can make monsters into saints, and the Crown of Thorns is there to remind us.

With the knowledge of such love, how can we not be troubled by our own lack of love? I recall a foreign government official on his knees, in tears, as he prayed before the relic. He was at the foot of the cross and did not want to leave the chapel that houses the holy relics of the passion. I can say that I am always moved to bring out the Crown and see young and old kneel, touch, and kiss this relic of our salvation. Their veneration is a thanksgiving.

Among the dignitaries who have done so in recent years have been U.S. President Barack Obama, the Prime Minister of Russia Dmitry Medvedev, and U.S. First Lady Melania Trump. I know that Vladimir Putin carries a desire to kneel before Christ, the redeemer of humanity.

Every first Friday of the month, at three in the afternoon, and every Friday of Lent, as well as on Good Friday, when the Crown is venerated all day long at Notre Dame, a great assembly of people participates in a "holy hour" that often becomes two hours because so many faithful keep coming. For years, we church ministers have neglected to foster popular piety in our pastoral care. What a mistake that is!

What do I mean by piety? Originally describing the virtue of the duties of religion and its influence on the whole life of Christians, the word *piety* has gradually taken on a more general sense, sometimes used to refer to someone who is praying or the context in which prayer happens. Today, expressions such as "exercises of piety" or "feelings of piety" don't mean much. "Popular piety" is considered a second-rate piety. I understand the limits of such piety and that we must re-evangelize it. It can become superstition, a form of paganism.

Shepherds of souls, especially those who serve at popular religious sites, ought to accompany the faithful. Far from being a secondary quality to be dismissed, and even less an escape, piety is an essential aspect of Christian spirituality. In Christ, humanity is called to offer spiritual worship, filial homage to God of "what is good and acceptable and perfect" (Rom 12:2).

I often meditate on this passage of John's Gospel: "We declare to you what was from the beginning, what we have heard, what we have seen with our eyes, what we have looked at and touched with our hands, concerning the word of life" (1 John 1:1). At Notre Dame, the faithful hear and see and touch the word of God. Some bring pictures of their children or pictures of people who are sick to ask for healing. What testimonies of faith! Yes, these little ones teach us a lot; everything is simple and clear. After praying, after wiping their tears, their faces radiate, as though touched by the grace of salvation. In preparing the meditations for the holy hour, I often think of all these faces, sometimes suffering, but which come to exhibit such peace, echoing Psalm 80:

> O God;
> let your face shine, that we may be saved. (v. 3)

The canons of the Cathedral could testify to it as well as I can.

From time to time, I welcome representatives of the media who wish to do a report or documentary on relics. I had no idea, when I arrived at Notre Dame, that I was going to receive so many requests so often by media outlets. Fortunately, a few years ago, I received some "media training" on the occasion of "Paris Toussaint 2004," an evangelization training event organized by the archdiocese. We all know the dangers of working with the media, of course—narcissism becomes such a temptation. But we also know how important it is that the church is present in the media. There are two good reasons for me to cooperate with reporters: to increase awareness of the Cathedral and the resulting increased interest of people in coming here to visit and pray. If it's for our personal glory, it will bear no fruit. We must beware of superstar priests who risk losing their souls. I'm not suggesting that I should live in hiding, but only that I must be cautious to do my duty and no more. The media can become a drug! The allure of the camera—which you're not supposed to look at. The microphone—you must master it, practicing what you want to say seven times before saying it, even though media training says practice three times.

Let's get back to the subject of the Crown of Thorns. I'm sure that the fervor of those present before it in prayer always amazes the commentators, camera operators, sound technicians, and producers who come to the Cathedral.

I never forget that Mary is the queen of the house. After Pope Francis called for the Monday after Pentecost to be celebrated annually as the Feast of Mary, Mother of the Church, I organized, with the team of chaplains, a Marian procession on the square that day, just as we do for each Feast of the Assumption, on the evening of August 14 and again on the afternoon of August 15. The silver statue donated by King Charles X on August 15, 1826, which is in the Cathedral treasury, is carried on the shoulders of the Knights of the Holy Sepulcher, followed by a crowd that sings the "Ave Maria" in alternation with dozens of rosaries. What a beautiful expression of popular piety this is, where we pray not only with our hearts, but also with our feet!

The archbishop presides over the evening Mass after Vespers. Expecting that first time to celebrate the Mass in front of a small gathering, he was overjoyed to find his Cathedral full! His simple homily touched hearts; he reminded the faithful that, at the moment of death, there is usually a written will. Jesus, too, left a last will and testament. And what did he give us? His mother. Beautiful wisdom of the heart. I saw believers weeping, expressing both suffering and abandonment to the one who, because she is a mother, takes care of each one of us with tenderness.

Every Saturday, the rosary is recited in front before the Virgin of Paris, and each Marian feast is celebrated with solemnity, especially December 8, the Feast of the Immaculate Conception, which brings together the canons and seminarians. On the Feast of the Presentation, February 2, we celebrate especially with the canons and the religious men and women.

The feasts punctuate life at Notre Dame. As I have already said, I like to pray at the foot of the Virgin of Paris, who sometimes offers concrete signs of her care. One day, I spent time with a group of Dutch high school students who wanted to spend some time in prayer with Mary; they wanted to pray for one of their teachers who had committed suicide. They brought his photo, and we placed it at the base of the statue. After I led them in prayer, I asked if any of them had any prayers they wanted to say aloud. One of them showed me a prayer they had found in their teacher's classroom; it was Paul Claudel's beautiful prayer, "The Virgin at Noon." But the students didn't know who had written it or who Claudel was. How moved they were when I explained to them that the author of the prayer had experienced his conversion in the very spot they were standing! This was a nod from Mary to all those young people, who are not about to forget her after that. They had arrived with a burden in their hearts; they left with lighter hearts, sure that their teacher, gone too soon, was with them, in communion, at Notre Dame. A beautiful sign of hope and conversion.

On the Saturday before Pentecost, there is the traditional Notre-Dame de Chrétienté (Our Lady of Christendom) pilgrimage. Six thousand young people walk in pilgrimage from the Cathedral of Notre Dame in Paris to the Cathedral of Notre Dame in Chartres. In 2018, they carried a relic of the heart of Padre Pio, the great Capuchin saint who died in 1968 in San Giovanni Rotondo. This priest, who bore the stigmata, was a missionary of mercy. Persecuted by the church that did not believe in the supernatural phenomena he experienced, he always remained obedient. One day, while hearing the confessions of young brothers of his convent, the priest manifested symptoms of transverberation—his heart was pierced by a spiritual arrow, and he bled from a wound on his chest. His body is venerated in San Giovanni Rotondo, and he was canonized by St. John Paul II in 2002.

After the departure of the pilgrims, the heart of Padre Pio, preserved in a beautiful reliquary created by the famous French sculptor Goudji, remained in the Cathedral for the rest of the day. Many faithful came to entrust their intentions to him—families, infants with disabilities, the sick, the young and not so young, children, and elderly.

During the veneration, I held the heart of the padre on my heart. What did I ask him? To give me the radiant heart of a shepherd, like his. However, I told him that I could do without any stigmata! In short, I asked to be a father after the heart of Christ. I will never forget this opportunity to be so close to the heart of St. Pio.

Among the great processions we carry out, there is that for "fathers of families," which ends at Notre Dame with a Mass presided over by a bishop, followed by veneration of the Crown of Thorns. Two thousand fathers reflect on their vocation and sing the glory of God! Fortunately, stained glass is strong, because the voices of the men rise, and the organ carries them off! These are precious moments for the rector.

4

THE CONVERSION OF PAUL CLAUDEL

PAUL CLAUDEL—THAT IS, *Canon* Paul Claudel—has a special place in the history of Notre Dame Cathedral, since it is here that he experienced his conversion. An engraved plaque at the foot of the Virgin of Paris memorializes this spiritual event.

This prominent French poet, playwright, and diplomat was born on August 6, 1868, in a tiny village in northern France. After high school at the Lycée Louis-le-Grand in Paris, he enrolled at the Paris Institute of Political Studies, where he discovered the talents that he would go on to put to service in a long diplomatic career. Meanwhile, on the evening of Christmas day in 1886, at the age of eighteen, he experienced what he later called his "conversion." We'll return to that in a moment.

For over forty years, Claudel served as a diplomat in New York, Boston, China, Prague, Frankfurt, Hamburg, Rio de Janeiro, Copenhagen, Tokyo, Washington, and finally Brussels. A member of the French Academy, he was also recognized as one of the greatest writers of the twentieth century. His work includes the plays *The Tidings Brought to Mary*, *The Satin Slipper*, and *The Break of Noon*; the poetry *Five Great Odes*, a lyrical masterpiece;

and we can't forget his journals and his correspondence, which reveal his personality. He died in Paris on February 23, 1955.

But let us return to his conversion, with the help of a poem written in 1942, more than fifty years after the experience it describes. The text represents Claudel looking back at one of the most important moments of his life to give thanks.

"After all, you, my Lady, made the first move."[1] This is how Claudel begins, addressing the Virgin Mary.

He displays a marvelous audacity that recalls the gospel question, "Woman, what does this have to do with me?" Christ loves his Mother, and, in this expression, he is not being dismissive of her. On the contrary, Mary is the new Eve who, by her yes, participated exceptionally in the work of salvation.

And Paul Claudel is correct to say that Mary took the initiative. As rector of this Cathedral, I, along with all its chaplains and confessors, can testify that even today, Mary calls to the faithful who are out on the square but who dare not enter, and she calls to those thousands of tourists who pass by her statue standing upon the pillar inside as she looks on them with tenderness and affection. She is the queen of the house. This Cathedral is her house, and she wants to lead us to her beloved Son.

It was during Christmas Vespers that Claudel, one young man amidst a massive crowd, found himself pushed close to the pillar upon which the Virgin stands. His description of the liturgy shows that he was still a novice and was merely—as he says—"standing around" watching. He wrote,

> And the sanctuary in the middle lighted up with gold and
> linen, and the great carpet with the arrangement
> of celebrants gold and lace up to the altar,
> The ceremony sideways from my position and
> the lighting up of that group of people in white
> singing and accomplishing something during the
> hour of time.

Claudel was looking at the liturgy as an outsider. He wrote in the poem about what he saw and heard. He was struck first by beauty, like so many faithful who still come today for the beauty of the liturgy in this wonderful setting, a witness to the faith of those who built it. The solemnity, the priests, the altar servers—all are transfigured by the presence of the Lord.

While the liturgy unfolds in time, it transports us toward its source, toward the heavenly liturgy. The singing of the psalms that reaches the vaults of the Cathedral, the great organ that meditates on the melodies that have just been interpreted by the choir, the curls of incense rising—they all combine to point our gaze upward.

Claudel writes, "Our Lady, the Woman-Church, with cries, large with God, erecting Her own Magnificat!"

As we intone the Magnificat in the royal tone, the celebrant incenses the cross, the altar, and the Virgin of Paris; and God's holy people, with Mary, take up the song.

In his *Five Great Odes*, Claudel sings the Magnificat with the assembly:

> I am like a priest, clad in his ample robe of gold,
> standing before the lit altar, and only his hands
> and his face have the colour of humankind,
> And he gazes tranquilly, face to face, in the strength
> and fullness of his heart,
> At his God in the monstrance, knowing precisely that
> you are there under the texture of the unleavened
> bread,
> And that soon he will take You in his arms, as Mary
> took you in her arms,
> And, mingling with this group in the choir who
> conduct the office in sunlight and smoke,
> Will show You to the obscure generations who come,

> A light unto the Gentiles and the salvation of Your
>   people Israel,
> As you promised to David, being reminded of Your
>   mercy,
> And according to the word which You gave to our
>   forefathers, to Abraham and his seed forever.
>   Amen.[2]

Claudel takes us into this time of adoration in which he is offering himself to the Father through the eucharistic act of Christ; that is why he sees himself as a priest. What a beautiful way to express his baptismal priesthood!

But let's return to Claudel's poetic account of his conversion:

> And that wretched child I was!—Yes, myself, I
>   repeat!—what did I do to be so carried away?
> And whence comes the reservoir of powerful tears
>   which collapses? the wild cry and the heart which
>   suddenly is outside me?

Echoing the *Confessions* of St. Augustine, Claudel realizes the gratuity of grace! Why him and not the person standing beside him, just as close as he was to Our Lady's statue? He surely received the answer to this question the day he was born into heaven! But even if the Lord takes the initiative, the heart of each person seeks him; the desire for God prepares the way for God's own call. We are in the presence of a thundering conversion of heart; the tears are the sign that Claudel the seeker of God is now disarmed. His feet remain on earth, but his heart is elsewhere.

"All that I was is over! and all I learned in school is over!" he writes.

All certainties fall, and all ideologies and projects. His life no longer belongs to him—the Lord has seized him! Paul Claudel had previously learned some truths, but at Notre Dame, he discovered the One who is Truth. One who is so touched by grace can hardly resist such wild overflow of hope! The convert changes his point of support; by grace, simple optimism has become the virtue of hope. Claudel is present in the Cathedral, but his eyes are directed toward the kingdom. I often tell visitors that the building's architecture directs our gaze to its vaults and beyond. One's vision acquires another dimension: heavenly. The visible allows us to enter the Invisible; this is the genius of our cathedrals. That's why I like to say that no one leaves this place untouched by it and that so many of those who enter the building as tourists leave as pilgrims! Claudel continues:

> Nothing to do to ward off that eruption of Faith, like
> the world in the depths of my being!
> Nothing to do to stop that voice before the world
> was which says to me: you are mine!
> Nothing to do to fight the impulsiveness, like
> someone who splits himself open, of the beast
> who says: I believe!

Yes, Paul Claudel is right: there is nothing one can do! Claudel opened his heart and God rushed into it. The call is radical: *You are mine!* And the response is just as radical: *I believe*.

Claudel was certain that God, through the Virgin Mary, intervened in his life. He was no longer divided within himself; he rediscovered a unity of love and inner freedom. Love ineluctably brings one to God. So he can write, "So, my Lady, everything that has happened since, I can't help it, you are responsible!"

After describing his conversion, Claudel describes the consequences. For conversion is not enough; faith must engage one's whole being and way of living. Let's remember that this text is from 1942; its purpose is to look back at the whole of his life under the gaze of God, to understand his path and his choices, not to mention his mission as a Catholic writer.

> All the groping search I have tried to carry out from one end of the world to the other through a terrible disorder and relentlessness and filth!

Certainly, Claudel is referring here to his diplomatic career and the great achievements it included. But he also refers to the compromises, interests, silences, fears, unspoken truths, and—as Pope Francis would say—worldliness of his life.

Claudel recognizes in the world traces of God. He remains a seeker of God, with a fiery zeal; the fullness of truth will be in the face-to-face encounter. But all our spiritual life is nourished by these little lights, these divine sparks that remind us that we are led by God.

The discoveries are many:

> The groping search all alone through the glory of
> God's justice!
> The questioning with the Mother of the Father we
> have in heaven,
> The questioning with the world, and with all that is
> and with sin.

Is this not the story of sin that each of us lives? Is it not the experience of redemption? In a century still marked by Jansenism, Claudel connects divine glory and divine justice. God is a just judge; he only wants to save. There is no vengeance in the heart of God!

Converted, one unfortunately remains a sinner, which does not prevent us from advancing toward holiness, despite or thanks to our history. This fragility that lives in us is a source of grace because "whenever I am weak, then I am strong," to cite St. Paul again (2 Cor 12:10).

> The questioning
> Of this Someone who when you push Him to the wall
> is not embarrassed by an alibi,
> And it's suddenly a smile for an answer in our arms
> of that child who leaves us defenseless and
> speechless!

How many objections, how many questions are put to the Lord in the face of the suffering of the innocent, in the face of evil, violence, death. And too often we find God silent. But the divine silence ends with a smile that disarms us. The divine smile that is reflected on Mary's face is a sign of God's tenderness, of his plan of love. It says, "You cannot understand now, but be patient. You will have the answers at the appointed time. There is a time for everything. Don't forget that I have been very patient with you as well."

We come to Claudel's conclusion:

> And so, if I have not done better, it is not my fault!
> And let me tell you that probably you would have
> done just as well to go to someone else!

Yes, God makes his choices! He chose Claudel and gave him the gifts he needed to accomplish the mission that God entrusted to him. Of course, it's easier for me than for Claudel to say that God made the right choice. But God's choices are always the best!

> All this paper I have piled up behind me is good for
> tears and laughs!
> If I had to reread it, you would see the face I would
> make!

There is always a separation between the writer and his work. As soon as his book is in the bookstore, it no longer belongs to him. The reader seizes it, not only to judge the novel, but to make it her own.

It is good to have a sense of humor about oneself and one's work. The great theologian Karl Rahner, at the end of his life, asked the Lord to let him come to the kingdom without his many theological works. Perhaps he was afraid of the content? But God has a sense of humor! What an abyss there is between our poor writings and the grandeur of mystery!

> Oh if it could come about that there might be
> between us an agreement,
> My Lady, that all I have done and all I have written,
> you might be willing to consider it as nothing at all!

Is this false humility? Not at all. When one is thunderstruck by the Lord, all that is not God becomes fragile. Claudel knows the price of grace, and he does not want to naturalize the supernatural.

Let us consider how he puts it in his fourth ode, "The Muse Which is Grace":

> You call me the Muse and my other name is Grace,
> the Grace that is brought to the condemned and
> by whom are trampled the law and the justice.
> And if you seek reason, it is not only that love that
> exists between you and me. It was not you who
> chose me, it was I who chose you before you were
> born. Among all living beings, I am the word of
> grace addressed to you alone.

Claudel is certainly a genius, but the word transcends him; it comes from God, because that is the mission of the Catholic writer.

Having learned in the school of the "little Thérèse," Claudel wanted, at the end of his life, to arrive before God empty-handed:

> And that I might come before you, blessedly intact
> and empty,
> Basically stripped of all my insipid literature!

Is it so insipid? We need Catholic poets and novelists. Great literature makes us dream and think. It expands our minds, even to the point of leading us to the supernatural. The vocation of Catholic writers is so important.

Again, Claudel realizes that his mission is impossible. How to express the Invisible? How to express the design of God's love? Fortunately, Mary came into his life, bringing true closeness to the Lord.

> Let me pause and collect my thoughts in the
> expectation of what will not fail to happen in a
> short time,
> Like someone to whom something terrible is going
> to happen—for example, raising his eyes and
> seeing you! and pretending not to be afraid!

This is Paul Claudel's spiritual testament. He shares with us still today the event that upended his life in Notre Dame Cathedral as a young man. His ultimate meeting with the Virgin was only a recapitulation of his life with her. She came into his heart on December 25, 1886, and she received it on February 23, 1955. And how astonished might he have been when he arrived at the door of the kingdom and was received first by the Virgin Mary, to whom he could then recite the words he once wrote:

It is noon...
I have nothing to give and nothing to ask.
I am here, my Lady, only to look at you...
Because you are there for always, simply because
 you are Mary, simply because you exist,
Mother of Our Lord, we give thanks to you![3]

At the beginning of this chapter, I called him Canon Claudel. Indeed, he is the only layman ever to be named a canon of Notre Dame Cathedral, and this dean of the chapter can only say, Amen.

But remember that the experience that this literary genius shared with us in his poem is only one of many conversions that have happened in Notre Dame Cathedral, but which will only ever be known in the hearts of those who experienced them.

5

NOTRE DAME, MOTHER AND TEACHER

TALKING ABOUT CLAUDEL brings us to an exciting subject: the question of the transmission of culture and faith. At first glance, this may seem like a very academic topic, worthy of a university lecture. But I'm convinced that it is an essential and even vital question.

For years we have seen the failure of so many great institutions—such as families, schools, and religions—to transmit to a new generation the most important aspects of what they are about. This is also the case regarding culture, a problem that threatens the future of a society or even a nation. Indeed, a society that fails to transmit its values, its culture, and its history ends up forming only barbarians.

My interest here is not to indulge in nostalgia, but rather to invite us to reflect on the notion of culture, including the question of its origins. Allow me to begin with two great figures of Christianity who witnessed the end of Greco-Roman civilization. The first is perhaps its greatest genius, St. Augustine, bishop of Hippo. The second is his friend St. Jerome, the founder of biblical exegesis.

We see in these two men two different responses as they watched the walls of civilization collapse. Jerome panicked.

Upon the invasion of Rome by the barbarians, he fled the city and went to a cave in Bethlehem, accompanied by a few friends. Augustine, who had never believed in the permanence of civilizations, regarded the future by noting in *The City of God* that what must remain will remain and will span the centuries, serving as the foundations of new civilizations. This is a beautiful description of tradition, which is never simply repeating what those who came before us have said, but rather imitating their creative daring.

Applying this description to the situation today, we are challenged to adopt an attitude of openness to what is new, rather than to close ourselves up in a desire to protect our culture at all cost. This is not about a battle between the ancients and the moderns.

So how do we promote the dynamism and expansion of a new culture without losing our living fidelity to the legacy of tradition? This question becomes particularly acute when it comes to harmonizing the culture that is the fruit of the remarkable development of science and technology with classical culture, bringing together different traditions. A society that rejects its cultural heritage will regress and become dehumanized.

We must pause here to think about the notion of culture. One might think of exercising our bodies as a sort of physical culture, but for the spirit or the soul, there is intellectual, spiritual, and moral culture. And having never been much of an athlete, I'm better able to discuss these. Culture is a characteristic of human life, to quote the Angelic Doctor, St. Thomas Aquinas. This means that the human person lives a truly human life through culture. Each one of us, in fact, becomes who we are thanks in great part to the culture in which we grow. It gives us our language, our imagination, our customs, our sensibilities, our prejudices, our history, our art, our science and technology, our ways of understanding the world. It gives us our heritage and our rights, including that every person must have access to culture and that every person plays a role in it and carries the burden of the responsibilities that it imposes. In the broadest sense, the word *culture* refers to everything by which a person refines and develops the multiple capacities of his or her mind and body. As such, human culture necessarily has a historical and social aspect, and the word *culture* often has a sociological and even ethnological meaning. In this sense, we can talk about the plurality of cultures.

St. John Paul II, in a 1980 address to UNESCO (the United Nations Educational, Scientific and Cultural Organization), noted, "Culture is a specific way of man's 'existing' and 'being.'"[1] It is the human person and the person alone who is expressed by and in any culture and who finds in culture his or her balance.

We can say further that to grasp the origin of culture, we must recognize the human person as the bearer of unique and independent value, of transcendent dignity. Culture must be subordinated to the integral development of the person, to the goods of the community, and to that of the entire human race. This means that it requires a just freedom to flourish and a legitimate autonomy of action, in accordance with its own principles.

Starting from this foundation, we can make a few observations.

First, education is an essential task of any culture. I am not saying anything new by noting that the crisis in education, which did not emerge yesterday, is troubling. I do not want to venture into the basics of learning to read and its impact on spelling skills; other competent institutions have taken the measure of the disaster. But what I'm sure of is that our young graduates have a hard time reading and understanding a text, and sometimes those who grade what they write have to read their words out loud in order to understand what the student meant! Writing and language are the essential tools to engage in any culture, and they are of fundamental importance for the formation of interpersonal and social relationships. We must beware of this disjuncture between today's young people and adults! I know the phenomenon of group or tribal thinking is involved here, too. But if our words no longer have the same meaning, we will be moving toward misunderstandings that will sooner or later lead to violence.

I'm not talking about suppressing the work of the academicians who find themselves having to expand and revise the dictionary now on an almost weekly basis. It is not a question of saving outdated or obsolete words that mean nothing to anyone today. But neither can we abandon the richness of our French language or lose the subtleties that are the joy of linguists and of foreigners who are passionate about the beauty of our language.

Unfortunately, we are witnessing a shift toward education in a very narrow sense of the word. It is understood to be solely at the service of getting what we think we must possess, rather than making us the kind of person we ought to *be*. Or, in other words, education is at the service of *competition* and not *communion*. This undermines equality of opportunity.

Perhaps we must see in this the consequences of our technological revolution, which is not always at the service of the human person. The French author Georges Bernanos pointed out this risk more than sixty years ago:

> The tragedy of nineteenth-century Europe...is just man's inability to adapt to the new life rhythm, the beat which can no longer be measured by his own heart-beat but only by the dizzy spinning of the turbines racing ever faster and faster....But has the Machine World made men better? Has it made him more humane?...We are not witnessing the natural passing of a great human civilization, we are witnessing the birth of a new, inhuman civilization which can only be established by a vast, an immense, a universal sterilizing of the higher human values of life.[2]

This is, of course, not a question of condemning technological progress, especially if it is at the service of humanity, but to draw attention to a utilitarian drift that leaves no room for freedom. What place is there today for poets? Claudel, referring to Dante, noted,

> The object of poetry is not, as some suggest, dreams, illusions, or ideas. It is sacred reality, given once and for all. It is the universe of visible things, to which faith adds that of invisible things. The *poësis perennis* does not invent its themes, but always takes up those that the Creation provides—just as our liturgy does, and we don't grow tired of that, any more than we do of the annual cycle of seasons. The aim of poetry is not, as Baudelaire says, to plunge "into the depths of the infinite to find something new," but rather to plunge into the depths of the definite to find the inexhaustible. This is the nature of the poetry of Dante.[3]

Second, I want to note the link between nation and culture. I don't want to jump into the debate on national identity here; I leave that to politicians. But I want to affirm that every nation exists through culture and for culture. A nation's strength and identity lie in its culture. Some nations have struggled to maintain their culture, their own values. During a visit to Syria, I met the Syriac Catholic Archbishop of Aleppo, who told me of his concern about the diaspora of Syriac Christians. How will they celebrate their liturgy? Will they lose it? Forget it? Behind these questions is another: What future does it have? The archbishop saw clearly that, since the Syriac liturgy is part of their culture, a failure to hand it on could lead to the disappearance of this group. The same is true of the presence of Christians in the East.

My third remark regards memory. It is wrong to think that everything in the development of human history is at the mercy of change and that there are not, throughout history, things that remain permanent.

It would be an irretrievable loss for knowledge and for culture to think that the past has ceased to have meaning and value for us and that only what is modern has meaning. If the French writer Albert Thibaudet was correct when he said that culture is memory—that is, if culture allows us to hold on in every age to humanity's great works of the past—then to see meaning only in the modern would be the very negation of culture. If ideological, political, and economic systems are merely a reflection of their times, if they become outdated and replaced by others with the passing of time, there still are permanent truths that we must hold onto. There is truth in Plato or Aristotle that withstands the wear of time. Works that reflect sociological circumstances are prone to the erosion of time. But those that express the depths of humanity, some aspect of what is essential to being human, are as young today as they were when they were first created or expressed. We still recognize the greatness of the prehistoric painter who drew the figures on the walls of the cave. The philosopher or the poet who achieves certain resonances, harmony with what is essential, is no longer at the mercy of history. If these works fall into oblivion, we would experience a crisis of knowledge, a kind of barbarism. Our civilization would no longer be a culture, but the very negation of authentic culture.

We should give thanks for our prestigious museums, which are not just the reflection of a past, but places of the *transmission* of culture, where young people discover what their ancestors created, not from nothing, but by allowing themselves to be enriched by the achievements of their own predecessors.

I dare to tell you this: I have always enjoyed teaching classes with the help of various works of art, either while standing in the presence of the originals in a museum or by using reproductions of them in a classroom. For example, I have explained the play *Phèdre*, by the great seventeenth-century playwright Jean

Racine, by focusing on the theme of the sea and the sun, which allowed me to make a connection with the work of the painter Claude Lorrain, a master in the art of backlighting who brilliantly depicted how the sun interacts with the sea. Far from classicism, Claude delights in light and has a baroque style. One could also draw connections between the poetry of Jean de La Fontaine and the paintings of Nicolas Poussin, who perfectly integrates his people with his landscapes. We can't understand very well the work of the writer Jean de La Bruyère without appealing to the paintings of peasant life by the three Le Nain brothers. Nor can we understand Denis Diderot if we do not have before our eyes the fantastical ruins of Hubert Robert! Even less can we grasp Diderot's popular side without the help of Chardin's still lifes. Likewise, the philosopher Jean-Jacques Rousseau can be illuminated by the self-portraiture of Rembrandt, Van Gogh, Cezanne, or Gauguin. I'll end my classical litany there, but it reveals to you some artists and authors who formed me.

I can already hear the reaction of some teachers: "How can we explain such authors? When our students and sometimes even we ourselves don't know what grace is, or Jansenism, it is impossible to explain Pascal or Racine." Or the reaction of some parents: "What good is all of this going to do them?" And I answer without hesitation that culture cannot be understood at the level of practicality and effectiveness, but rather at the level of being and vitality. The scholar Ernest Renan liked to say that "a whole host of special data learned more or less painfully fades from students' memories. But we must be careful not to think that means their studies were for nothing. Because the intellectual culture that has resulted from the effort, the development of the mind that happens through such studies, remain, and that alone is worth the price."[4]

This process of opening humanity to the noblest values of the true, the good, and the beautiful is necessary for artistic creation to happen. Culture fosters an interiority that helps us assimilate what we read, see, or hear. In a world where everything is accelerating, we live far too much on the surface of ourselves. But the human person needs to go to the depths of her being to discover the gifts that can be put at the service of creation.

There is therefore a balance to discover, or to rediscover, if we want to transmit culture—to preserve the meaning of quality, the meaning of genius; to awaken admiration for deep moral, aesthetic, spiritual values; and in this way to reach the heart, not mere sensibility, but the inner person.

What ultimately constitutes a culture are the spiritual values it expresses. This means that the Cathedral has a vital role to play. It does not replace families or schools, but it still is a tool for the transmission of culture, as it always has been.

In what ways is culture transmitted at Notre Dame?

Let's start with the wonderful altar servers. Most of them are young students; their service becomes for them a school of liturgy. Certainly, one must learn to navigate the sanctuary and understand the elements of the liturgy. But this is not enough. To be a great server presupposes living the liturgy. I therefore offer the servers training evenings on the mystery of the liturgy, the spiritual life, what it means to be created in the image and likeness of God and with a desire for God.

Their service at Notre Dame is also an ecclesial school because the servers are recommended to us by their parish priests. And it is a school of obedience because one does not choose one's function in each liturgy; that is assigned by the liturgy director. It is a school of commitment and availability because there are so many liturgies that so frequently call for their service. But it's not a sweatshop! It is a joy to serve the bishop and to contribute to the beauty of the liturgy. It is a school of vocations; over the years, many of our great servers have gone on to enter the seminary and become priests. The liturgy draws us in, and I give thanks that some of the servers have taken up the priestly ministry. Of course, the formation we give is one of interior freedom. But to be near the altar, to serve the archbishop, naturally raises the question of the priesthood; it is up to each one to decide whether he hears such a call and whether to answer it.

After the Sunday liturgy, the servers join the clergy, the organist, and the master of ceremonies for a meal. These times of conviviality strengthen the communion among us all. Believe me, the rector's table is not dour! After spending long hours in the Cathedral, such a moment of relaxation is indispensable. Every liturgy requires a personal investment.

Another means of transmission is the association of volunteer guides called CASA (the Communauté d'Accueil dans les Sites Artistiques), already mentioned in chapter 1. In summer, these young people are present in the square outside the Cathedral to welcome and invite visitors. And they are not simply tour guides. They are committed Christians, and the visits they lead are cultural ones; they make the stones speak. And at their heart, the visits they lead are spiritual. In our pastoral jargon, we would say that they offer an implicit evangelization. Most tourists no longer know the vocabulary of the Catholic "tribe," so we must provide explanations. These visits are not catechism lessons, but privileged moments where grace can act.

These young people come to us and live in community for a month. Sent by their universities, they come from all over the world. It is an incredibly rich experience of learning community life. They all speak French, and they all are passionate about the architecture of our Cathedral. It is a privilege for these young students to share their passion. As in all kinds of teaching, if the teacher is passionate, her pedagogy is effective and learning is joyful.

I recall showing a group of American bakers around the Cathedral one evening after closing time. We got along well, since I do not go to McDonald's or eat their burgers, even if they have exotic names like the "mustard ranch beef"! I prefer a ham and butter sandwich on our French baguettes. The visit was therefore relaxed, which did not stop us from talking about the history of France, the goodness of God, and Mrs. Trump. At the end of the visit, as we drank Coca-Cola, one of them said to me, "When you retire, you can go into theater." I said the rector was already a good comedian because to take on all the tasks of my role, you need a good sense of humor. A sad saint is a bad saint; we shouldn't wear sour expressions, but happy ones. This is what attracts and evangelizes. If we exude boredom, we will scare away all who come to seek God.

But let's go back to the young people of CASA, who spend their vacation time doing this essential service. Thanks to them, many tourists can take the time to sit down and discover the mystery of Notre Dame. The cardinal told me once that he receives many letters from tourists who write to say that the Cathedral impacted them deeply. These young people, like all teachers, give back what they have received, not by repeating memorized lessons, but by sharing what gives them life. The Cathedral transmits culture and spirituality, and it enables others to transmit it. As we well know, the entire building is a catechetical picture book. One can spend hours contemplating the three rose windows with binoculars: on one side, the anticipation of the Messiah; on the other, the incarnation; and, at the end—as Cardinal Vingt-Trois described it—"the epilogue, the end of the waiting, the burst of light, the realization of the promise, the testimony of the universal Church....God is light. Infinite Love."[5] As the sun sets at the end of the day, this "rose" changes color. The reds start to sing, and the blues soften. Contemplating it offers a hint of the joy of the end-times.

When walking through the Cathedral once with the First Lady of France, I nodded to this rose window and said, "We are a people on the move—but here we walk toward the kingdom of God."

School children also come to discover the Cathedral with the help of educators who transmit the beauty and the richness of this mother church. Their visit provides a beautiful illustration of the cathedral builders of the Middle Ages and the history of our nation that they have been studying in school. Here again, Notre Dame carries out, as it has done for centuries, the beautiful mission of transmission. All these young people see a church that is alive with liturgical celebrations and many faithful praying in the different chapels.

It is time to turn our attention to other means of transmission, the Notre Dame choir and the educational and spiritual events that we offer here.

6

NOTRE DAME AND ITS CHOIR

WE CAN'T TALK about Notre Dame Cathedral without also talking about its choir and music school, known as the *Maîtrise*, a beautiful tradition that has been part of its life for centuries.

As a former choirboy, I want to begin by recalling Canon Jehan Revert (1920–2015), the tireless leader of musical life at Notre Dame over the course of several decades. Indeed, he not only directed the choir but also organized concerts and organ recitals with the great master Pierre Cochereau.

At Canon Revert's funeral in 2015, I said, "When a loved one leaves us, when a person who has deeply marked our own lives has just experienced his Passover, we carry in our heart some images that allow us to remember and especially to give thanks. But for us Christians, what is most essential about him is now in the Invisible, that is, in the Heart of the Father." I would like to offer a few of the images of Father Revert that I carry.

My first meeting with him took place in Rome fifty years ago, at a congress of the Pueri Cantores. He directed the five thousand young singers who gathered from many countries and did everything to avoid a cacophony that would have been unworthy of the Holy See! His friendly, expressive, and tender—but also authoritative—approach allowed all the children to give the best of themselves.

The second image is Father Revert in the Cathedral. As music director from 1959 to 1991, he put his gifts at the service of the liturgy. It is impossible to forget that warm voice that proclaimed the word of God.

Just as he lived so much of his life in the Cathedral, Notre Dame lived in him. He knew its vaults, its pillars, and even its bells (there is even a ringtone named after him, which made him smile!), and he made them all sing with the help of the choir and the organ. We can't fail to mention his friend Pierre Cochereau or Canon Émile Berrar. All three of them helped to make the life of the Cathedral what it is.

The third image I hold dear is Father Revert the liturgist, who intelligently and expertly applied the reform called for by the Second Vatican Council to liturgical music. His rich repertoire was remarkable. He was passionate about the liturgy and eager to allow beauty to nourish prayer. He taught children to sing, but what he brought especially was that extra spirit that touched the hearts of those who came to this beautiful Cathedral.

My final image is that of Father Revert weakened by age, sitting in his choir stall in the back—a humble priest who knew how to obey the church he loved so much and who lived his years of retirement in confident peace because he believed in merciful love. Despite his weakness, he remained ready to help and always kind. Grounded in his Marian spirituality, he went on foot every Thursday to the train station, where he took the train to Noisy-le-Sec, his family home, praying the rosary while he walked!

And now? I hold still another image, this one found only in my imagination, but I dare to imagine it, because of Canon Revert's smile. Yes, this is an image of Jehan Revert standing before all the angels of heaven, his arms raised, leading them in song: "*Sanctus! Hosanna in excelsis Deo!*" This is how he continues his work. After celebrating the liturgy for more than seventy years on earth, he has joined the heavenly liturgy. The angels and saints are surely happy to sing under his direction.

Today, the *Maîtrise* at Notre Dame is rooted in this tradition. It includes children in both Catholic and public schools, middle and high school students with arranged hours, and a choir of adults in professional formation.

Its primary mission is to provide music for the liturgy: Vespers every evening, lauds on Sunday morning, the 6:15 p.m. weekday Masses, and the Sunday Masses, as well as special diocesan celebrations, such as diaconal and priestly ordinations, confirmations, the Rite of Election for catechumens, and more.

Let's linger a few more moments on the topic of liturgical music. When we listen to Bach or Mozart in our Cathedral, we experience a bit of the glory of God. The mystery of infinite beauty penetrates us and makes us experience God's presence in a tangible way.

Pope Benedict XVI offered some guidelines for liturgical music to meet the expectations of the faithful. First, it must highlight the word of God. Let's admit that in the liturgy we've used hymns with lyrics that fall far short of this simple principle! We forget that our songs, springing from love, respond to the love of God. This does not prevent us from creating new ones. The Cathedral has regularly commissioned new compositions for the choir.

Also, knowing how to pray and therefore how to sing before God is a gift of the Spirit. The Spirit inspires music that *lifts up our hearts*, to use the words we say before the preface of the Eucharistic Prayer. This is a far cry from songs that are bellowed and have created generations of deaf people!

Let us not forget that in the liturgy we participate in the heavenly worship. In this beautiful setting, sacred music helps make the faithful aware of this. Those who come to the liturgies of the Cathedral seek beauty. This is what they tell us. And the musicianship of the choir does not prevent the active participation of the faithful—quite the contrary. It lifts our prayer; and if what attracts us first is aesthetics, our hearts are quickly transported to the kingdom. We receive many letters testifying to this, thanks especially to our Catholic television station, which allows us to reach those who are often alone or can no longer participate in the Eucharist because they are sick or elderly, or because there are not enough priests.

The young people of the *Maîtrise* are accompanied by a chaplain who offers them liturgical insights related to the music they will perform; Msgr. Maillet, the founder of the boys' choir known as the Les Petits Chanteurs à la Croix de Bois, established this essential element. These young people are not professionals, though some of them will one day go on to be. They are there to receive an integral human formation; this school forms the heart, mind, soul, and body. They don't simply offer a musical performance; they put their hearts into it and that is why hearts are touched by their interpretations. Musically, it's perfect. But the rector wants more than that in the liturgy; it is essential that the music help us lift our spirits to God.

Celebrating liturgical services in the Cathedral with the *Maîtrise* is truly a joy. Their cooperative spirit, encouraging looks, and smiles are always heartening. There is no competition between us—quite the opposite. The same is true of our organists—I like to congratulate and thank them at the end of the Mass, in the name of all the faithful present. A good understanding between us is necessary for the harmony of hearts. We can share such a relationship because we are on the same wavelength, and that's fortunate because the choir provides its services in about a thousand liturgies each year.

Each Sunday Mass has its own musical "flavor." For example, the "canon" Mass, presided over by one of the canons of the

Cathedral, features Gregorian chant. In these, the choir interprets pieces that were written for Notre Dame Cathedral in the thirteenth and fourteenth centuries. It is a pleasure for many people who love Latin to be able to celebrate such a Mass at Notre Dame according to the Missal of St. Paul VI. Though I was involved in implementing Pope Benedict XVI's *motu proprio* that gave broad permission for the celebration of the Mass according to the Missal of St. John XXIII, I appreciate the fact that the Second Vatican Council did not abolish Gregorian chant or the use of Latin, and so such liturgies are offered according to the Missal of Paul VI as well.

The 11:30 a.m. Mass is polyphonic; the choir performs works by Palestrina, Mozart, or some of the many other great composers. Visitors expect a beautiful liturgy. The rector makes sure that they get it. The mother church of the diocese must carry out the vision of the archbishop. To be sure, the Cathedral's musical program is not like what one finds at a typical parish, but Notre Dame is not a typical parish. We have around four hundred regular faithful; the rest are people visiting from around France, foreigners, lovers of beautiful music, organ enthusiasts who come from all over the world, and passing tourists whom the Virgin Mary has drawn inside and who leave moved.

The liturgies at the Cathedral also call for particularly beautiful vestments. The Cathedral has exceptionally beautiful modern vestments that, in such a setting, enhance the grandeur of the mystery. Nothing is too beautiful for the Lord. This does not prevent me from wearing for a major celebration items like the cope given by Napoleon III—though such vestments are heavy and difficult to manage.

The Cathedral has a beautiful treasury that includes many important and ancient liturgical items and that draws many tourists. But we only use these items for the most important feasts, such as Christmas, Easter, Pentecost, the Assumption of Our Lady. When the rector wants to indulge a bit of spiritual greed, he will choose an especially beautiful chalice to use at Mass! This is an opportunity to pray for those who have donated these remarkable pieces of goldsmithing. As I've said, the Cathedral is not a museum. Each archbishop has his own liturgical objects. Cardinal Lustiger entrusted to the sculptor Jean Touret the creation of the present main altar. Cardinal André Vingt-Trois used the chalice and ciborium donated for the 1997 World Youth Day in Paris. Popes St. John Paul II and Benedict XVI donated the chasubles they wore during their liturgies at Notre Dame. The rector is always moved to wear them—and enjoys them because they are light.

Let's say a bit more about the *Maîtrise*, its singing, and the formation its young members receive.

First, the formation is not easy; this is how we form the will. Members learn to be on time, be attentive, work on the scores, listen to those around them so as not to overpower their voices. One mustn't scream; each voice is a treasure, an instrument. They are "normal" young people, but ones who embrace the rules in the interest of developing their talents. They are not traumatized by the rigor—far from it. And when the rector shares a treat with them, they dig in as if they had not eaten for eight days! The formation we offer is not about creating "stars," but young people who learn how to use their talents for the greater glory of God.

Besides the liturgy, the Cathedral also offers concerts. Each Tuesday evening, the *Maîtrise* offers a high-quality program that attracts many tourists, but also lovers of great music. They represent a beautiful cultural aspect in the life the Cathedral, the city of Paris, and France. For events like these, the police often help to ensure the safety of the square, the Cathedral, the archbishop, and the rector.

For the Feast of St. Lucy, we have a concert each year in connection with the nation of Sweden; celebrating this feast is a major Swedish tradition. One year I had the joy of welcoming King Carl XVI Gustaf and Queen Silvia. This visit, of course, required many preparations. Not only was it necessary to ensure safety, but also to respect protocol. The Cathedral was visited by police dogs checking for hidden bombs, then completely closed and scoured by the royal security team. Everything about the visit was carefully planned. We met with officials to prepare for the event and, to avoid any diplomatic incidents, I studied the essential protocols because I'm no specialist in the proper ways to address nobility and royalty! "His Royal Highness," "Your Majesty," "Madam"—one can get lost! (As it turns out, you start with "Your Majesty" and then you can say "Madam.")

As we prepared to enter the Cathedral together, I was standing at their sides. The king does not speak French, so of course the conversation was brief. However, Queen Silvia possesses admirable command of the language. So we chatted about Pope Francis and all the young singers in the choirs, one French and one Swedish. Then we walked up the nave. The spectators rose; the Swedish community was trying to catch sight of Her Majesty. But she did not stop, did not extend her hand, except to the rector, when they arrived and when they left.

Sitting in beautiful red armchairs, we listened with joy to our two choirs. Between pieces, the queen shared with me how impressed and moved she was. At the end of the concert, the king and queen rose to sign the guestbook, then presented a gift to the Cathedral. After that, I led the royal couple back to their official car, which was escorted by police motorcycles.

Everything went so well that the following year we welcomed the Swedish Prime Minister. I still did not know Swedish and the Prime Minister did not have his interpreter, so the conversation was short. Fortunately, music fosters harmony among people.

For a more recent St. Lucy celebration, the Swedish ambassador to France was the guest of honor. A few days beforehand, he joined the archbishop of Paris to light the Cathedral's Christmas tree, which was given that year by his country. A beautiful tradition.

The rector has a diplomatic life! He responds to invitations and receives ambassadors who come to him with questions about France and the behavior of the French. During the 2019 "yellow vests" crisis, for example, I received an ambassador from a Latin American country who did not understand the violence, nearly two years after the election of our president, which had generated high hopes. Like any good diplomat, I explained that the French were difficult to govern and that there were real expectations that had not been met.

From time to time Bertrand Delanoë, the retired mayor of Paris, likes to come to Notre Dame for concerts. He had a role in the creation of the Sacred Music office, and the City of Paris, like the State, financially supports our *Maîtrise*. Our sacred music program serves as an ambassador of France and its capital.

The rector doesn't attend all the concerts. But each concert begins with a spiritual presentation by either a chaplain or the rector. The Cathedral's prestigious setting provides the backdrop, and the sacred music unfolds, carrying away all who are in attendance. The rector is spoiled; he no longer needs to go to the Paris Philharmonic, because he has all the beautiful music he could wish for right at home! A love of music and singing ought to be an essential criterion for appointment to this position I now hold—among other things, of course!

Besides the concerts, there are organ recitals every Saturday at 8:00 p.m. Organists all over the world want to come and play on this instrument of more than eight thousand pipes. There is a long waiting list, and it is the titular organists who make the selections. Not everyone can play on this great 150-year-old organ, which, with five keyboards and 109 stops, is the most important organ in France and probably the most famous in the world.

This masterpiece creation of Aristide Cavaillé-Coll was a beautiful gift to Notre Dame, completed in time for the Christmas celebrations of 1867 and dedicated on March 6, 1868. The titular organist post has been held by many great musicians, including Louis Vierne, Marcel Dupre, Léonce de Saint-Martin, and Pierre Cochereau, the latter known for his improvisations!

Today, we have three titular organists: Olivier Latry, Philippe Lefebvre, and Vincent Dubois.

For the instrument to be operational twenty-four hours a day, an organ builder employed by the Cathedral provides all necessary maintenance. The invited organists and the rehearsals take turns from 7:30 p.m. until midnight, which does not prevent the workers from making progress on the Cathedral renovation project, because any work that requires scaffolding is done only at night, out of concern for the safety of the thirty thousand visitors on the site each day.

And we should also mention the choir organ, which has thirty stops and eighteen hundred pipes, used daily for the Vespers services and evening Mass. Yves Castagnet is the titular organist. With a close relationship to the choir, he is its privileged partner. Since 1988, Yves has composed, accompanied, and prepared the musical aspects of liturgies. He was joined by Johann Vexo in 2004.

Reflecting on the role of the liturgy at Notre Dame, Cardinal André Vingt-Trois wrote,

> The liturgy is the living soul of the Cathedral. It is the place where the Christian people, gathered around its archbishop, celebrates the blessings of God throughout the days and sometimes nights. Throughout the seasons of the liturgical year, which reflect the seasons of the Cathedral, the spiritual and musical

> rhythms are linked with the light of the sun and the length of the passing days....The faithful, the regulars, the pilgrims, and the visitors are gathered in, through their senses and their hearts, to the liturgy that is celebrated, borne on the shoulders of the Good Shepherd who offers the praise of humanity to the Father of Heaven.

The rector enters into this great tradition of the sacred times and seasons of Notre Dame. The archbishop has entrusted him with this treasure. It's up to him to continue to enrich it with the help of the talented musicians who work and minister in this landmark of spirituality.

Organ recitals open to all can be privileged moments of evangelization. Hearts are touched, and grace does the rest! It happens when visitors take the time to sit down, listen, and see.

7

PREACHING AND TEACHING AT NOTRE DAME

THE SUBJECT OF THE long history of preaching and teaching at Notre Dame brings to mind first of all the annual Lenten sermons. Some great figures have had a place in this history.

The famous preacher Father Henri-Dominique Lacordaire (1802–61) preached the Lenten sermons of 1835 and 1836, reflecting on the church, its necessity and its authority, then on tradition, Scripture, and reason. The purpose of these talks was simple: to provoke conversion and repentance. Father Lacordaire offered further sermons from 1848 through 1851, presenting the Christian mystery in the form of apologetics, an approach that will remind many of the catechisms of their childhood.

Other great figures have preached at Notre Dame—renowned priests and preachers like Pierre Sanson, Alfred Baudrillart, Henry Pinard de La Boullaye, Michel Riquet, Ambroise-Marie Carré, Jean-Miguel Garrigues, Jean-Louis Bruguès, and Jean-Robert Armogathe as well as the renowned cardinals Joseph Ratzinger, Christoph Schönborn, José Policarpo, Péter Erdö, and Godfried Danneels.

Beginning in 2005, these sermons took a new direction, breaking with the tradition of a single preacher. Cardinal

Lustiger wanted to promote a dialogue between Christian faith and contemporary thought, as an echo of the work being done at Collège des Bernardins.[1]

These sermons are broadcast by the public radio station France Culture, by Radio Notre-Dame, and by the Catholic television station KTO. For that reason, many of the faithful now prefer to stay in their living rooms, listening or watching from their own armchairs, so fewer come to the Cathedral. I remember Lenten sermons so well attended that we had to sit on the steps of the sanctuary, and yet even then they were being broadcast live on France Culture.

We shouldn't be afraid of asking ourselves whether what we offer meets the needs of the faithful today. I'd have to admit that the content of some sermons through the years have been complicated and that you would almost need a philosophical dictionary close at hand to help you understand them!

Preaching is a difficult genre that mixes rhetoric, doctrinal content, and spiritual exhortation. We must read the signs of the times. Today, the faithful appreciate Pope Francis's homilies because they are accessible; they are a pastor's words that touch the hearts of the faithful.

Lent has always been for Catholics a special time for being called to conversion through good preaching and teaching.

We need a new apologetic because the Catholic faithful, even many of those who are most engaged, do not know the content of the faith anymore. Young people no longer understand "the language of the tribe." I remember talking once to a group of children about parables, but I soon realized they were struggling to see the connection between Jesus and the satellite dish on the roof of their house.[2] On a different occasion, after I had talked to a group of high school students about the cardinal virtues, one of them asked me why I had spent so much time praising the virtues of the cardinal who runs the archdiocese! And once at the seminary, during a lecture on the Council of Trent, one of the seminarians was convinced we were talking about the thirtieth council![3]

These little examples show us that if we don't want the church to become a new Tower of Babel, we must do something different. Here again, we are talking about the question of the transmission of faith and culture.

Together with the Cathedral chaplains, I recently proposed to the archbishop a new approach that fits well in the tradition. We suggested a series led by one preacher, a priest of Paris, on a theme that is the heart of our faith: the resurrection of Christ and our own.

I have always thought that the Cathedral, the mother church of the archdiocese, should feed the faithful and pilgrims. This is done through preaching, but also through spiritual lectures given on Sundays.

That's why soon after I began my post, I organized a series of talks, in connection with the Cathedral school. These talks are moments for spiritual rejuvenation that allow us to renew our reception of the mystery of Christ by drawing on the insights of theologians, spiritual leaders, and artists, in a climate of meditation. Teaching theology is a joy for me because it allows me to share what gives me life. The primary mission of the rector is to transmit "the joy of the gospel" through liturgy, teaching, cultural events, concerts, encounters in the heart of divine mercy.

It takes time to write these thirty-minute talks, which are broadcast live on KTO. I choose all my words carefully, and that takes work, but I don't mind doing it. They are the fruit of my forty years of ministry. I have often done a lot of teaching and preaching, especially for the Lenten series on France Culture or preaching retreats. So I have gathered a lot of material to work from. But I can't just rely on previous work because the people who hear it are different each time, and it's important to respond to their needs.

Our use of YouTube helps me understand what people are looking for. Thousands of people have viewed the talks.

The most popular were the ones on the Our Father, Thérèse of Lisieux, Georges Bernanos, following Christ, and finally, priesthood in the teaching of Popes John Paul II, Benedict XVI, and Francis. These latter ones were undoubtedly more theological.

It's not a matter of simply trying to get big numbers. I don't know how many people are watching—I just know that there are about a hundred and fifty people in front of me at the Cathedral as I'm speaking.

The needs are spiritual; the faithful want simple, solid teaching that relates to their lives.

I've also noticed a desire to rediscover great Catholic writers, like Bernanos. Some listeners told me they had read or reread *The Diary of a Country Priest*. The lecture I offered on Bernanos was both spiritual and theological, a former literature professor juggling the ideas of a great writer. Among the listeners was Bernanos's son Jean-Loup, who told me he'd discovered from my talk facets of his father's work that he had not realized. Hearing that was a great joy, but I immediately commented that a teacher has a way of putting words in an author's mouth, so maybe Bernanos himself would be amazed at his own spiritual depth!

On the occasion of the 150th anniversary of the birth of Paul Claudel, I offered a series of three lectures on his work. Many people attended, including his grandson François Claudel. Following my comments about Claudel's plays *The Break of Noon* and *The Tidings Brought to Mary*, François told me with tears in his eyes that he was astonished at my interpretation of his grandfather's work. I told him that his grandfather might be astonished, too.

Preparing and presenting these conferences helps the rector maintain his own spiritual life and his own internal equilibrium. Rereading St. Thérèse is a good *lectio divina* that helps one to pray. The first beneficiary is therefore the rector; likewise, when

I prepare the Lenten series for France Culture, or any preaching, I am evangelizing myself first.

I never repeat homilies I've given in the past. The word of God is alive, and how it touches our hearts depends on what we are experiencing at any given time.

I have the reputation of preparing my homilies well in advance. I've always liked to keep well ahead of my work schedule, even in high school. That's probably a reflection of my manic side, or just a desire for planning ahead! In any case, it is extremely useful for my ministry in the Cathedral, where it's hard to juggle all the official duties.

The anxiety of sitting down to the blank sheet of paper—what a delight! Though some will think that the rector is a bit old-fashioned, I admit that I'm unable to write in front of a screen—it paralyzes me. Fortunately, I am lucky to have the help of a faithful nun who has been assisting me for years and types all my texts. The miracle is that she manages to decipher the chicken scratches of my handwriting.

The first line is always difficult, then the tip of the pen begins sliding across the paper. It stops, crosses out, pauses, begins again, until it gets to the end of the page. Writing is a real relaxation for me. Some people go to the movies, others spend time on social media; I choose to write. It's a way of creating that is not always easy, especially at the moment of birth!

Preparing for a retreat is a lot of work. There are thirteen 45-minute talks to prepare. I do that work in my library-office, surrounded by my books. It requires silence or a background of classical music, an atmosphere that helps me think and work through my memory to recall references, files, or previous talks. I never start from nothing, after all.

Preaching a retreat is a retreat experience for oneself, too. The rector makes sure to take time for himself, to retire to a quiet place to be alone with the Lord. A retreat allows you to eat well, sleep well, pray long, and walk in nature.

Finally, my homilies are the fruit of prayer and *lectio*. It's a difficult art. A homily should be short. It needs to start with a *captatio*, an image that touches the heart, especially a homily offered to the faithful at Notre Dame! But the faithful are often visitors or tourists; fortunately, there is a core group of people who come faithfully. The tourists often don't understand French. To get a sense of the assembly, I tell a little story to see if there is any response! Thank God, there are French speakers at Mass.

Sometimes people ask me, "How can you write your homilies so far in advance? What if, in the meantime, some event happens that changes everything?" I answer, "If Christ returns, I won't have to preach—we will be in glory! And if the pope passes away, there will be time to add a paragraph."

The fact that a preacher writes his homily doesn't mean he should simply read it aloud when it comes time to deliver it—that would be deadly boring. A good preacher must make sure to maintain his own freedom in relation to his text. But he knows the beginning and especially the end. There's nothing worse than homilies that are unprepared. This art presupposes personal work; a preacher who tries to just improvise ends up offering a homily that is a wordy waste of time, empty piety, boring, or merely a paraphrase of the gospel.

Preaching at Notre Dame is a challenge; we know that the faithful want to receive an insight that will nourish them throughout the week ahead.

You must be a little theatrical, you must love to preach, but, above all, you must be willing to work at it!

With this chapter, I conclude the first part of this book, on the pastoral ministry of the rector. This is the foundation of what will follow; it is the source that gives me life.

Part Two

LIKE RUNNING A SMALL BUSINESS

8

BEING "THE BOSS" OF A SMALL BUSINESS

IT'S NOT ALWAYS EASY to be both a priest and a boss! I mustn't mix up the roles or fall into a paternalistic attitude toward the staff at Notre Dame. As soon as I arrived, I met with each one of the Cathedral's sixty-seven employees. Naturally, this was quite different from hearing a confession! But I wanted to tell them that before anything else, I was a priest and that I would lead this "small business" as a happy priest, while aware of my responsibilities as a boss.

Because the Cathedral lives solely on donations, prudent management is important. I have to think about paying wages and bills at the end of every month. I must also participate in the life of the diocese by helping parishes on the east side of Paris that lack the financial means to support their own pastoral ministries. As a former vicar general who worked directly with these parishes, I can attest to the importance of their presence and their work. Christians in these difficult neighborhoods are signs of communion. The church is a source of life there, the presence of God who welcomes all people of goodwill. Having made many pastoral visits there, I've always been amazed by the work of the parish priests and their communities of faith. They are missionaries in the heart of their neighborhoods. How many examples of this I hold in my memory!

I recall, for example, encountering a religious sister I knew sitting in Buttes-Chaumont Park. She was taking care of a small child to give his mother a chance to run an errand. A simple thing, but it's the kind of gift that touches hearts. Or the building manager who was surprised to hear tenants who were far from the faith ask him, "Pray for me," because his office, with all his statues and pious images, resembled a chapel!

There is no need to go to the far reaches of the world to do missionary work; it's urgently needed in our own city. When the archdiocese built St. Luke Church in Paris's 19th district, a Muslim woman offered a donation to help build on this beautiful site. She said, "What a joy it is to see that there will soon be a church in our neighborhood—it was lacking that!"

We are no longer in the time of the catacombs. We must dare to show ourselves in the world, not in order to say that we are the best, but to let the world know what gives us life and gives meaning to this world that is so often disoriented.

I remember making a pastoral visit to the parish of St. Bernard de la Chapelle. I got off the metro and emerged onto the street a little lost, trying to find the church. Many Muslims live in the neighborhood, and in fact I found myself in the middle of a colorful market that reminded me of a souk in Tunis or the market in Libreville, with the smells of spices filling the air. A man called to me, "*Abouna*"—"Father" in Arabic—"what are you looking for?" I replied, "St. Bernard's Church." He took me by the hand and led me to the church. Thank heavens for my Roman collar, which helped that kind man—a Muslim respectful of the role of a priest—reach out and help me find my way. What an amazing image it must have been to the people in the neighborhood: a priest being led by a Muslim man to find a church!

But let's return to our topic—my role as "the boss" at Notre Dame.

What is my day like? I'm present for the opening of the Cathedral at 7:45 each morning, after having sung lauds with my brother priests in the rectory. The opening of the doors is solemn, a little like at the Holy Sepulcher in Jerusalem. The doors are so heavy! At that point the cleaning, which began at 5:30 a.m., is coming to an end, even if there are some nooks and crannies still to be cleaned up, because the staff knows that the rector is a little manic and that he will come in by morning.

The doors are opened to welcome the first pilgrims and tourists. The Cathedral is silent. The rising sun illuminates the windows of the sanctuary. The sacristan prepares for the celebration of the 8:00 a.m. Mass in the Pietà chapel. A few latecomers hurry in for Mass. At this Mass we find mostly people who work in the offices nearby, or just early birds who know that the future belongs to them. A visit to the Cathedral at this time of day is pure joy. On this day, I'm meeting a journalist from France Culture who is reporting on art in cathedrals; we meet at 8:00 a.m. near the crowned Virgin, and we speak of the silence and the words that spring from all these magical stones! An amazing radio show where silence is heard.

After saying good morning to the arriving staff, including the Cathedral supervisors who are getting ready to welcome the thirty thousand daily visitors, the sacristans, and those who do the housework, I get to my office next to the Cathedral, on the first floor.

Above my office is that of the administration and finance director; we meet every Monday morning to take stock. Assisted by the management controller, an accountant, and the payroll manager, she keeps me informed about income and expenses. Business regulations develop quickly, and I need good help to continue being a good and just employer.

My strength is to trust those around me. The administrative work is heavy, and the rector can't do everything. I am aware of the efforts required. This confidence allows me to prepare my homilies and conferences, receive those who want to meet with me, in short, to accomplish the pastoral tasks so important for my spiritual well-being.

I am assisted by a finance council, made up of financial and legal experts. They are not there to keep watch over me, but to give me advice on management and encourage me. The council makes sure that the donations we receive are used first in the service of the Cathedral's pastoral mission, and it helps us avoid financial problems by keeping a check on any grandiose projects the rector might dream up. (They need not worry about the latter—being attentive to the Cathedral is enough for me!)

Since my arrival in September 2016, the council has approved the installation of lights in the chapels, the establishment of a chapel for the Chinese and another for the Poles; the *Dame de Coeur* light show; new wooden display stands for the candles; new dispensers of medals bearing the images of Notre Dame, the crowned Virgin, and Popes John Paul II, Benedict XVI, and Francis; a more state-of-the-art sound system; and all the regular projects that keep the Cathedral both beautiful and well maintained.

Between my appointments, staff members don't hesitate to approach me about various issues or questions. Everyone knows that my office is open, but everyone also knows that I respect and trust our staff—that's the best way to avoid the discord that the devil loves.

As in almost any business, there are staff representatives, an important body that allows me to keep a good sense of the workplace climate. These representatives are elected within the union, and the boss should keep his nose out of that activity. Our meetings happen in a healthy atmosphere, and we appreciate one another's work. Of course, when you're working hard there is always the potential for tension or conflict, but the goal is to defuse the bombs before they explode!

Of course, people are people and problems arise. The rector then takes the time to invite conversation, listen, and defuse the atmosphere. I don't enjoy conflict, but it arises at times, and we must face it. That's why I like to "hang out" in the Cathedral. I have always favored personal contacts, outstretched hands, a smile, attention given to everyone.

We must know how to encourage those we work with, especially those who are in sensitive positions, such as security. The law does not allow them to stop someone who might be creating a scene in the Cathedral or a pilgrim engaged in some overly distracting mystical ecstasy. These things are rare, of course, but anything can happen. As Pope Francis says, you have to be ready for surprises.

The security personnel are there to help ensure that all visitors have a pleasant experience in the Cathedral and, believe me, this is not an easy task, since more than thirty thousand people visit every day. Some tourists who are used to speaking loudly—their culture, apparently—do not lose this habit when they enter Notre Dame. On the contrary! With earphones stuck in their ears to listen to the guide, their camera running, their hats on their heads, and emotions high, they sometimes shout their words to those nearby, though it's hard to understand why. Sometimes giving them a little "shhh!" gets no response, and offering a little gesture can help a bit. But still they continue. They're in another universe and don't understand how to behave in a church. This is certainly a tiresome job for the supervisors, but also for the rector who, at Sunday Mass, hoping to create a prayerful atmosphere, tries to quiet all these groups as they enter one after the other. It's interesting to sometimes see them quiet down noticeably when they encounter a chapel that relates to their own nation or culture—for example, the Chinese chapel—making them feel a little bit at home.

The staff who work in the reception area, the Cathedral treasury where many sacred objects are displayed, and the gift shop also help to foster this climate of interiority and mystery. Staff must deal with all kinds of questions offered in many different languages. Meanwhile, they also have to attend to things like answering phone calls, distributing headphones, helping those who are lost, calming people who get upset—it happens!—and directing people to the confessionals where they can talk to a priest.

In 2018, Notre Dame was named by TripAdvisor as the most welcoming tourist site. This could only happen thanks to the work of all these people. One must know how to respond without laughing at astonishing questions, like "Where is the drop of milk from the Virgin Mary's breast?" or "Is the statue of Joan of Arc's mother here?"[1] Apparently, what is metaphysically impossible is possible in the church!

Below the Cathedral, a gift shop offers books on Notre Dame and objects of piety, like rosaries, medals, crosses, and statues. Tourists like to take home a souvenir of their visit; some faithful like to take advantage of the shop to buy gifts.

Of course, I have received letters telling me that I should chase the moneychangers out of the Temple, like Christ! I answer that the shop is located discreetly in the basement and that the income we receive from it allows me to pay the employees and to maintain the building. Indeed, the money is used to take care of essential aspects of the life of Notre Dame, like the sound system, welcoming visitors, heat, and electricity.

On the other hand, everything related to worship is taken care of by the church. Money from votive candles, donations, bequests, and gifts are an important part of our income. They are what is used to pay the priests. Strictly speaking, the priests receive no salary; they get a ministerial allowance. Each priest receives the same allowance, about one thousand euros per month, and their housing and laundry are also provided.

At Notre Dame, we have two cooks who spoil us, one during the week and the other on weekends. There are usually between five and ten of us at table—a beautiful moment without mobile phones to distract us, where we can freely talk about what we've been reading, the news, or our theological research. Our priestly community supports one another. As I write this, we are ten happy priests, between the ages of 52 and 91. We pray together, but we also go out together for activities like the theater, a movie, or a riverboat tour of Paris. Yes, we sometimes have fun.

Every Wednesday, we meet to discuss and divide up the pastoral tasks and for reflection on our projects of evangelization. But above all, we pray midday prayer, then read the following Sunday's Gospel reading together and share some ideas for our homilies.

These fraternal relationships impact the life of the Cathedral. Each of us likes to be there, especially on weekends, to encounter the thousands of people who visit. This is a place inhabited by a priestly presence, and that can only bear good fruit. We each have different personalities, and that's good. Each brings his own experience, and the rector is there to foster communion. It is Our Lady who touches the pilgrims who come to pray at this important spiritual site.

In line with the pastoral priorities of Pope Francis, we welcome many people who have the desire to put their lives under the merciful gaze of the Lord. A priest is not there to judge, but to help penitents accept their sins and advance in holiness. The confessional is not a place of psychological torture, but a place where the heart opens; what a grace to allow oneself to be seen by the Lord! But we must be careful—the penitent must not confuse the priest for a therapist, and the confessor cannot pretend he's a "shrink," even if he has some understanding of psychology.

Such a confusion of roles does no one any good. I remember at the end of one meeting with someone, she asked me how much she owed me. I told her, "Here's your bill: two Hail Marys and three Our Fathers." Spiritual guidance is free because it is first God's work, the work of grace. The medicine of souls can be as complex as the medicine of the psyche. We are interested in consciences, souls, hearts. We do not try to untie psychological knots; we entrust them to Mary, who undoes knots. It is also true that the priest can refer the person to a psychologist when he perceives a problem that he can't solve.

Besides the priests and the employees, there are about twenty volunteers who welcome visitors. They play a vital role, distributing the liturgy sheets, accompanying the disabled, helping the faithful to find an empty seat, and all this with a smile and kindness. Volunteers are very much in demand because they are present at each liturgy. They are part of this beautiful family.

I perceive my role as leader to be a craftsman of communion. Counting employees, volunteers, and those who provide security and cleaning, we number around one hundred.

I might have liked to have been orchestra conductor, but no one can do everything! But that is the sort of role I play now. Sometimes there are cacophonies, but my job is to help avoid them. I prefer human relationships. While e-mails are useful for asking questions or providing answers, excessive use of these tools dehumanizes us. The screen is a barrier. We must help our young people learn to use all these screens wisely. It seems to me that we all need to learn a little more discernment about how to make sure these technological tools *serve* the work we're doing, rather than *become* the work.

Every month, I study the balance sheets, especially in relation to the budget. But it's not enough to do only that, because there is another, much more spiritual tally that would be easy to miss: that of grace. The rector doesn't seek to make a profit for the Cathedral, either in the sense of finances or in the sense of numbers of the faithful; such numbers are only a barometer. Certainly raising money and seeing many visitors is encouraging for everyone, but what matters to the rector is creating a place where grace can work within those who visit.

My joy is a young person approaching us to ask for baptism. It's the person who once walked in a tourist and became a pilgrim here and now asks to be married here in this place where the Virgin once called her. It's a young man who hears a call from the Lord, or a sinner who finds the joy of becoming a *forgiven* sinner. My joys are the many encounters with people when I circulate in the nave, all those who work to protect and enhance the beauty of our Cathedral, and my brother priests who come to celebrate here with groups of faithful. I love priests, and I have always been attentive to accompanying them spiritually. My joys are the liturgies that I prepare for my archbishop to celebrate, as well as all the liturgies over which I preside: Vespers, Masses, processions, and so on.

The reason I offer such a litany is to illustrate the importance of striking a balance between the role of priest and that of employer. My close associates know it well. It's a hard balance to maintain, but it's important to maintain it.

The rector's days begin at 7:30 a.m., but they don't end at 7:00 p.m.! There are official visits, embassy receptions, concerts at the Cathedral, spiritual vigils, organ recitals, spiritual reflections, and rare moments to visit with family and friends. But I remain available to them all. I always feel blessed when I finally get home for dinner and finally bed.

And on my days off, what am I doing then? Those are rare—that's my fault, of course! Is that a good idea? No, of course not. On the other hand, I spend one month each summer in Val-André in Brittany, where the air refreshes me. I was brought up to know the value of hard work and effort, but that was...in the 1960s!

I began this chapter by saying it's not always easy to be both a priest and a boss; I conclude now by confiding that it is also a real joy to be both a priest and a boss, provided that I never allow these two roles to become completely separate. It is a matter of pastoral chastity; that is, the closeness I have with all employees is a pastoral element, and it must be balanced with a distance that preserves my freedom as a manager. This is particularly true in moments of conviviality, like at Christmas, the Twelfth Night meal, or the end-of-year celebration organized by the staff. The latter is a barbecue in the rector's garden—when the firefighter is posted next to the grill, not for tasting, but to prevent the Cathedral from catching fire. Everyone participates in joy and relaxation. Journalists from France 2 who were present recently for one of these enjoyed seeing the hidden face of the Cathedral, discovering the presence of laypeople and priests who know how to have fun and relax.

9

VICTOR HUGO'S NOTRE DAME

WHEN I LEFT MY assignment at St. Francis Xavier parish, I was spoiled with gifts. The parishioners had given me a beautiful statue of the risen Christ. The priests of the parish gave me the manuscript of Victor Hugo's *The Hunchback of Notre Dame*. No, it was not the original, but a wonderful reproduction! This manuscript helps to reveal how the writer worked. The rector has read Hugo often, including this epic story that suggests some ideas for bringing life to the square in front of the Cathedral.

As a teacher, I have taught many of the works of this great visionary with such a rich vocabulary! Let us linger, for a chapter, on the one that inspires me when I am on the square before the Cathedral, contemplating its magical facade.

Hugo finished his long novel in early January 1831. He wrote it in six months. But for three years before that, he had studied a great deal—chronicles, maps, inventories. He had explored the Paris of Louis XI and what was left of its old houses. Above all, he learned the Cathedral thoroughly—its spiral staircases, its mysterious little stone rooms, its ancient and modern inscriptions. He wanted everything in his novel to be historically accurate—the decor, the people, the language.

In fact, while the details are real, the characters are quite surreal. The archdeacon, Claude Frollo, is a monster. Quasimodo is one of those hideous dwarfs with big heads that populated Hugo's imagination. And Esmeralda is more of a fantastical vision than a woman.

There is something of Victor Hugo in Claude Frollo, torn by the struggle between desire and his vow of chastity. There is something of Pepita and Adele[1] in Esmeralda—her brown skin with that golden reflection of Andalusia, her black eyes, and her slender waist. There is Hugo's essential theme of the triple rivalry, among the gypsy, the archdeacon, and the hunchbacked bell ringer. A reader who knows Hugo well senses these secret correspondences; invisible and powerful, they animate the novel.

But the true protagonist is "the vast Church of Notre-Dame which, with its two towers outlined in black against a starry sky, its stone sides and its monstrous hip-roof, seemed like some huge double-headed sphinx crouching in the heart of the town."[2] Hugo had a gift, in his prose as well as in his drawings, for throwing strong light upon his subjects and putting them in front of a background populated by strange and dark shadows. Capable of loving or hating inanimate objects, he lent an extraordinary life to the Cathedral and to the city.

The novel is not a Catholic book nor even a Christian book. Many were shocked by this story of a priest devoured by desire and love for a gypsy street dancer. Into the wall of the Cathedral, Frollo carved the Greek word *Anankè*, meaning "inevitability," rather than God's Providence. "Fate, you vulture, do you grasp the human race?"[3] Burdened by hatred and hurt by the disappointments of friendship, Hugo's own answer was yes. A cruel force reigned over the world—illustrated in the tragedy of Esmeralda, an innocent and pure girl, caught in the web of ecclesiastical tribunals. Supreme *Anankè*, the inner destiny of the human heart!

Perhaps also, in an echo of his time, Hugo reflected the

anticlericalism of the day, with a "this will kill that...the press will kill the church...all civilization begins with theocracy and ends with democracy" that was typical of the era. Alphonse de Lamartine, another noted writer of the day, reproached Hugo, saying of *The Hunchback of Notre Dame*, "It is a monumental work. It is the Shakespeare of the novel, the epic of the Middle Ages. But it is immoral because of the absence of Providence. You have everything in your church except a little religion."

What does it matter! Hugo displays the breadth of his imagination and his verbal power. He has the most expansive vocabulary of our language; he loves to work with words—he uses six thousand different ones in this novel. He uses them to seduce, to take hold of the reader's ear. It is the same skill that brings such color to his poetry.

Reading or rereading *The Hunchback of Notre Dame* helps us discover Paris, crowded and colorful, with its slums populated by disturbing criminals and its Cathedral whose imposing Mass comes alive with a mysterious and fantastic life, a mixture of the sublime and the grotesque, in the person of Quasimodo in particular.

The plot is simple. It is 1482, and the poet Gringoire is lost in the Paris slums. His life is threatened, and he is saved by a beautiful gypsy, Esmeralda. Archdeacon Frollo feels a sinister passion for her and orders the bell ringer of Notre Dame, Quasimodo, to kidnap her. But Captain Phoebus saves the girl, who then falls in love with him. For his attempted abduction, Quasimodo, a deformed monster, is sentenced to be pilloried. But moved with pity, Esmeralda gives him a drink, and the poor man falls for her. But Frollo murders Phoebus and allows Esmerelda to be convicted of the crime. She is brought to the square in front of Notre Dame for her death sentence to be carried out. But Quasimodo intervenes and takes her into the Cathedral, where she will enjoy the protection of the law of sanctuary. Gypsies invade the building to help their friend, but the bell ringer fights them off. I'm sure you are familiar with the violent and grandiose scene where Quasimodo defends both Esmeralda and his Cathedral from the intruders.

How can we not recall—perhaps while sitting on the square, as the sun sets at the end of the day, throwing fiery colors upon the facade—a few lines of book 10, chapter 4:

> Anyone who had seen Quasimodo at that moment would have been frightened. Besides the projectiles which he had piled upon the balustrade, he had collected a heap of stones on the platform itself. As soon as the missiles at the edge of the railing were exhausted, he had recourse to the heap below. He stooped and rose, stooped and rose again, with incredible activity. His great gnome-like head hung over the balustrade, then a huge stone fell, then another, and another. Now and again he followed a particularly fine stone with his eye, and if it did good execution he said, "Hum!"[4]

Victor Hugo, through his use of the rhythm of words, helps us imagine Quasimodo's movement, and, one can imagine, his agitation—the cruel gnome shouting in victory after killing one of the attackers. But he is one man against many, and he hears the great doors of the central portal creak under the force of a battering ram.

> The ragamuffins were not discouraged. More than twenty times already the heavy door which they were attacking had trembled beneath the weight of their oaken battering-ram, multiplied by the strength of a hundred men. The panels cracked; the carvings flew in splinters; the hinges, at every blow, shook upon their screw-rings; the boards were reduced to pow-

> der, crushed between the iron braces. Luckily for Quasimodo, there was more iron than wood.[5]

Let's take a moment to consider the doors of the Cathedral. Hugo knew them well, and this is clear in the description he gives of them. The visionary Hugo emphasizes through his text the strength of Notre Dame. In a last effort of defense, Quasimodo quickly melts down a pile of lead grout and hurls it down upon the assailants:

> All at once, just as they gathered together about the battering-ram for a final effort, every man holding his breath and straining his muscles so as to lend all his strength to the decisive blow, a howl more frightful even than that which had risen and died away from beneath the rafter, again burst from their midst. Those who did not shriek, those who still lived, looked up. Two streams of molten lead fell from the top of the building into the very thickest of the throng. This sea of men had subsided beneath the boiling metal which had made, at the points where it fell, two black and smoking holes in the crowd, as boiling water would in snow. About them writhed the dying, half consumed, and shrieking with agony. Around the two principal jets there were drops of this horrible rain which sprinkled the assailants, and penetrated their skulls like gimlets of flame. A leaden fire riddled the poor wretches with countless hailstones.[6]

This is Hugo in full form! We see the Cathedral become chaotic, and the author concludes his story with an image:

> All eyes were turned to the top of the church. What they saw was most strange. Upon the top of the topmost

> gallery, higher than the central rose-window, a vast flame ascended between the two belfries with whirling sparks,—a vast flame, fierce and strong, fragments of which were ever and anon borne away by the wing with the smoke.[7]

I'll stop there! But one should reread this story and come to Notre Dame. There are sometimes even students studying this novel in school who come here asking for a "Victor Hugo tour" of the Cathedral. These stones affect people, and the literary brilliance of this great novelist helps.

Thank you, Victor Hugo, for having brought attention to this Cathedral, which was in poor condition in your day, due to age and lack of maintenance. He was the only one to denounce this scandal. Is it not the mission of the poet to revive our heritage? In the preface of Hugo's *Odes et Ballades*, we find these words:

> It is especially to repair the evil done by the sophists that the poet must toil today. He must walk before the people as a light that shows them the way....He is to be the echo of no other word but God's. He must always remember what his predecessors too often forgot—that he too has a religion and a homeland. His songs will ceaselessly celebrate the glories and misfortunes of his country, the austerities and raptures of its worship, so that his ancestors and his contemporaries can receive something of his genius and his soul, and so that, in posterity, other people do not say of him, "This one sang in a barbarous land."

How could we fail to recognize in these lines our Cathedral, an image of France and its history?

And in Hugo's poetry collection *Les Rayons et les Ombres* (Lights and shadows), we read,

It, despite thorns,
Envy and derision,
Walks bent in your ruins,
Gathering up the tradition.
From that fertile tradition
Comes forth all that covers the world,
All that heaven can bless.
Any idea, human or divine,
That has the past for its root
And for its foliage the future.

It shines! It throws its flame
Upon eternal truth!
It makes it shine for the soul
With a marvelous clarity!
It floods its light
Upon city and desert, Louvre and shack,
And plains and mountain heights;
To all it is revealed from above;
For poetry is the star
Which leads kings and shepherds to God!

10

FUNDRAISING

IN 1825, VICTOR HUGO published a pamphlet titled "On the Destruction of Monuments in France," in which he denounced the disappearance of medieval monuments. A few years later, his novel *The Hunchback of Notre Dame* helped motivate public authorities to save the Cathedral. In an article called "Stop the Demolishers," Hugo listed the great buildings that had recently been demolished in Paris and then concluded,

> It is time to finally put an end to these disorders, to which we call the attention of our country. Although impoverished by devastating revolutionaries, by mercenary speculators, and especially by classical restorationists, France is still rich in French monuments. We must hold back the hammer that is destroying the face of the country. A law would suffice; let it be done. Whatever the rights of ownership, the destruction of a historic and monumental building should not be permitted to these ignoble speculators with blind interest in only their own honor. They are miserable men, and so stupid that they do not even understand that they are barbarians! There are two parts of a building: its use and its beauty. Its use belongs to the owner, but

> its beauty belongs to everyone. It is therefore going beyond an owner's right to destroy it. Active surveillance should be exercised on our monuments.

Especially through the interest generated by his novel, Hugo became the first of the restorationists of this old Paris and more particularly of Notre Dame.

The building was indeed in very bad condition, and it was Eugene Viollet-le-Duc and Jean-Baptiste Lassus who embarked on the great work of restoration.

We owe a lot to Viollet-le-Duc: the repair of the drainage system, the replacement of damaged stones, the restoration of the west portal to its original state, the replacement of the lost statuary of the gallery of the kings, the restoration of the flying buttresses of the chevet, the rebuilding of the spire with the addition of Victor Geoffroy-Dechaume's three-meter tall copper statues of the apostles. How can we not mention the restoration of the statuary? Viollet-le-Duc wanted Notre Dame to look like a thirteenth-century cathedral, populated by fantastic creatures like chimeras, striges, goats, elephants, eagles, cats, and half-human, half-beast creatures. And we must mention, too, the construction of the sacristy, completed in 1853, which is now badly aged.

Well over a century and a half later, the weight of the years is heavy, and it is time to get to work. In the garden below the chevet, the fallen stones are numbered and waiting in a makeshift shed for patrons who will help restore them to their rightful place.

What are the priorities? The spire and flying buttresses.

Let's pause for a few moments to talk about Notre Dame's spire. The first spire was constructed around 1250. In 1792, it was removed due to decay. Then Viollet-le-Duc had it rebuilt; this spire is ninety meters tall. Inaugurated in 1859, it underwent a restoration between 1933 and 1935. At this point, the famous rooster was temporarily taken down. After two months of work on it, Cardinal Verdier blessed it and deposited in its gilded copper body a lead tube containing relics of St. Denys, first bishop of Paris; St. Genevieve, patron saint of the city; and one of the thorns from the Holy Crown. Then it was restored to its perch.

I can imagine already the emotion I will experience when I go up to retrieve the rooster for its next restoration.[1] Fortunately I'm not prone to dizziness, and there will be an elevator. As I write these lines, the scaffolding is being built. Part of our medieval masterpiece will unfortunately be obscured behind five hundred tons of it. The relics inside will be kept in the Cathedral until the end of the work.

We have already brought the statues of the apostles down because they too needed a good facelift.

How happy it makes me to see how attached the faithful are to their Cathedral—and not just Parisians! The maintenance of historical monuments is expensive. Where to find the money? Notre Dame Cathedral belongs to the French government, and therefore the Regional Directorate of Cultural Affairs is responsible for maintaining it. I first want to say that the Cathedral is well cared for. There is special attention from the Île-de-France regional government, which has been investing in its care for years.

Marie-Hélène Didier, curator of the Regional Directorate, supervises the restoration of religious objects and relics; she is very attentive to this work because she loves the Cathedral. Dominique Cerclet, general curator of Heritage, leads the work. Every year, the state invests two hundred thousand euros in it. Our relationships with these people and offices are excellent. The work involves plenty of reciprocal trust and wise cooperation.

When I arrived at Notre Dame in September 2016, I would not have used Victor Hugo's words, because Notre Dame was standing. But after discussions with the French chief architect of historical sites, Philippe Villeneuve, it seemed clear to me that it was time to tackle a new restoration effort. Unlike in the time of

Viollet-le-Duc, the church—that is, the Cathedral—is committed to participating financially in this important project. The cost will be 150 million euros. We will contribute 60 million of this—but we'll have to find it first!

A plan is developing, and while the church may have the words of eternal life, the administration of the state takes its time!

But the day finally arrived. The cardinal, the diocesan treasurer, the communications director, and I met at the Élysée Palace with President Hollande and the Minister of Culture. We signed a simple agreement: every euro the Cathedral gives, the state will match with another euro—up to 2.5 million per year. Which, if I'm not mistaken, comes to five million euros. We then found ourselves in the garden where we sipped orange juice together. This was two days before François Hollande left office.

While saying goodbye on the steps of the Élysée, the president wished us good luck in our efforts to gather the funds. I told him that I might have to do some belly dancing. "You'll have to learn how!" he replied. Did he really believe it? In any case, after one year, the total commitment of gifts from donors in France and the United States was more than three million euros. Challenge met! But this was just the beginning. The effort continues.

Our initial fundraising success has allowed us to begin the work for a period of at least five years. In that time, we will restore the flying buttresses, some of which are in very bad shape. All this work is entrusted to specialists and master craftspeople.

Again, the rector is the orchestra conductor! I set up a team looking for donors in France and the United States.

Why the United States? Simply because Americans love the Cathedral, a symbol of history that illustrates the deep Christian roots of France. I do not speak a word of English, so I rely on the language of signs: a smile, extended hands—and sometimes even a little kiss! During one of my quick visits, a Canadian woman told me, "You are Notre Dame," and she kissed me.

I replied that I was only the rector. "What does it matter," she added, and kissed me again. It's not always easy to be the rector of Notre Dame!

A tour of New York, Washington, and Boston was organized, to meet generous donors.

Again, why go to get the money from our American friends? It seems important to strengthen our bonds of friendship between our two countries, the Cathedral being a place where peace is built. Also, American tax laws are much more generous than ours in France.

This is a significant investment of the rector's time. After all, there are only twenty-four hours in a day! I thank each donor, whether their gift is five thousand or a hundred thousand euros. I must welcome special guests and provide them with tours of the Cathedral from floor to rafters. Mind you, my doctor asks me to get exercise; I do it on those stairs, though I can't find Quasimodo or Esmeralda!

As a former teacher, I always find it a joy to share what I am passionate about. I have the opportunity to do that for these exceptional and endearing guests.

Some people say to me, "Why not charge an entrance fee to the Cathedral? Raising the money you need would be so simple." The journalist Stéphane Bern made this proposal one day in the media. The response of the church was clear, and mine with it. Indeed, I went out of my way to defend the free access of visitors. I met with Bern and we were able to speak candidly. I explained that Notre Dame is a living cathedral, not a museum. I explained that a great many visitors are pilgrims rather than tourists and that distinguishing between the two at the entrance would not be simple. In short, my friend Stéphane tweeted after our meeting, "The rector of Notre Dame is a man of conviction, but also of dialogue."

Let's say a bit more, if you don't mind, about my objection to charging an entrance fee for cathedrals.

My first argument: Notre Dame is a place of grace, and grace is free. Having to buy a ticket at the door would change the attitude of one's heart while inside. It would feel like entering a museum. Of course, the visitor may have an aesthetic response, but will there be an encounter with the Invisible One? I recently went to visit the cathedrals of Avila, Salamanca, and Segovia—each had an entrance fee, except for the clergy. My blessed Roman collar allowed me to enter for free, but it did not open the doors of the sacristy so I could celebrate Holy Mass. There was no priestly presence—just a counter at the doors where visitors could purchase audio guides.

The entrance fee makes the visit feel like a cultural one, not an encounter with the Master of the place. We want a place of grace that touches the hearts, where visitors can meet the One they come to visit. The Cathedral is beautiful, but what makes it more beautiful are the living stones, the people who come to gather before the Virgin or in the Blessed Sacrament chapel or the Crown of Thorns chapel. It is a place of grace because God touches hearts—and that is how a tourist becomes a pilgrim.

My second argument: The Cathedral is alive. Every day within its walls, many celebrations happen—four daily Masses, Vespers broadcast by KTO, pilgrimage Masses, the availability of the sacrament of mercy for seven hours. And all that's not even mentioning various diocesan celebrations and other special events; the archbishop uses his Cathedral as the site of spiritual events and retreats. To treat the Cathedral as a museum would mean reducing the variety of celebrations that contribute to the grace of the place.

Allow me to quote Cardinal André Vingt-Trois, who served as Archbishop of Paris from 2005 to 2017:

> Liturgical celebrations are not some exotic activity that curious visitors come to witness. The liturgy is the very breath and focus of the ministry of any church.

> By living out the liturgical life at Notre Dame, we are not trying to create a certain atmosphere or to display some cultural artifact. We offer the living Christ free of charge, first of all for believers, knowing that, moreover, the work of Christ will provoke thought, belief, love, insight, and hope for those who experience it. In visits to many other sites, one must pay in order to be allowed to see. We want visitors at Notre Dame to be able to receive without paying anything. We want the Cathedral to be alive with the life of God.

My third argument is not the least of them: How can we distinguish tourists, whom we'd charge admission, from the faithful, whom we wouldn't? With a camera? Of course, tourists can be believers at the same time!

Let's listen again to Cardinal Vingt-Trois:

> Who are these people who stop by the tens of thousands each day to visit Notre-Dame? Are they pilgrims? Tourists? Visitors? Or ordinary passers-by? While some come explicitly for a spiritual visit because of their Christian faith, it is clear that's not the case for everyone. However, the mission that Christ has entrusted to us prohibits us from presuming that there is *any* visit without a spiritual component. It is our duty to welcome each visitor in the name of the Lord and to share with him or her something of the life of God.

It is impossible, then, to demand money from believers who seek an encounter with their Lord. I am told that in Italy or Spain there are sacred sites where you must pay to enter. But let us not forget that these cathedrals belong to the church, which needs the resources to maintain them. Unfortunately, many of these cathedrals have become exclusively tourist sites, rather than places of worship and prayer. As for me, I prefer doing fundraising to help the state maintain ours.

My fourth argument is about hospitality. We have our regulars who need a place to warm up on a cold day. So many poor people in the street find refuge in our churches, and Notre Dame must maintain this beautiful tradition. The Hôtel-Dieu,[2] built by the church, is there to remind us. There has always been, beside Notre Dame, this place of charity. Even if the Hôtel-Dieu is exclusively a hospital today, charity must always be present. The Cathedral is not overrun by homeless people, but they know that if they are too cold, they can come here and find human warmth.

My fifth argument is important, too; it is an economic argument. If the entrance fee is twenty euros, will many visitors then hesitate from making offerings inside the Cathedral after paying an entry fee that goes to the state? This would mean I'd be forced to dismiss a large part of the staff and thereby reduce all the pastoral activity that makes Notre Dame a place of grace.

My sixth and final argument is the law, established in 1905, that authorizes the church to carry out its pastoral ministry as it sees fit.

Let's not act like Don Camillo and Peppone.[3] I prefer intelligent cooperation to a political conflict that gets us nowhere. The Cathedral is a place of peace, just as its rector is a man of peace. That's why I proposed to work with Stéphane Bern for the safeguarding of our heritage, which is our shared passion.

Fundraising seems to be the best solution, even if it requires a lot of effort. But what effort should be spared to save a cathedral?

Indeed, in October 2018, on the Feast of the Holy Guardian Angels, I boarded a flight with the diocesan treasurer to New York City. For relaxation? No. I'm not fond of flying; I prefer to have my feet on the ground, in reality as well as in spirituality. We arrived at our hotel at noon, grabbed a quick lunch, then prepared for the first gala dinner where Notre Dame would be the topic of discussion. Before the dinner, I took a walk through the Broadway district. What a world! I felt crushed by the huge and impersonal buildings. Thankfully, the bright, multicolored advertisements reminded us that we were in the neighborhood of musicals, concerts, and other entertainment. But I was not in New York to sing, but to share my passion for that beautiful, 850-year-old Lady. In my formal cassock, I went to the residence of the French consul general. It was she who was graciously hosting us in her residence for this first meal that would bring together a group of potential American donors. Everything was planned to the minute.

At 6:00 p.m., we stood at the top of the stairs to welcome our guests. The convivial aperitifs helped us get acquainted. Not speaking English, I just smiled and thanked them for their presence. Thank God, some of these guests spoke French, and I felt less alone. But there was no time to waste. At 7:15 p.m., we entered a beautiful room transformed into a dining room, and madame consul offered some opening words. Then she gave me the floor. Here are the comments I offered, which were translated by the communications director:

> It is a real joy for the rector of *Notre-Dame de Paris* to be in New York to share with you my passion for this ever-dynamic Cathedral.
>
> When I arrived two years ago, I was alarmed by the state of degradation, including the spire, the chevet, the gargoyles, and the flying buttresses of the chancel. I felt a call to undertake this work. Without delay, I signed an agreement with the French government and agreed to cover part of the expense of restoration. Many French people are already offering their financial support, and I am thankful. The Cathedral is the most visited Parisian monument, a place of

grace where tourists and faithful can have a spiritual experience. I like to say that the tourist who goes in can become a pilgrim coming out.

Notre Dame recapitulates the history of France. It is still a place of communion today where the French, whether they are Christian or not, like to meet to confide their troubles, because it is a place of peace.

I know how much Americans are attached to this Cathedral that represents our friendship. So many faithful Americans like to come to pray, to listen to our choir and our organ. It is always a joy to greet them and thank them for their presence, a sign of the communion between our two countries. I had the opportunity to say this to your First Lady and your ambassadors. The Cathedral, with its history, belongs not only to the people of Paris or to the people of France; it belongs to the world. This is why Notre Dame is also your Cathedral. It signifies the friendship between our two nations.

You are always welcome for a private visit, so that I can help you discover, not Quasimodo, but the millennial treasures that are the very soul of our Cathedral.

On behalf of the Archbishop of Paris, I thank you for your important presence so that Notre Dame can continue its mission of peace. May the crowned Virgin protect your beautiful nation.

There was applause, and then dinner began. I was seated to the right of our host, and we talked about heritage, Stéphane Bern, and the Grand Palais. On the other side of me was a French banker who lives in New York. Echoing my speech, he explained that he is passionate about cathedrals, but that he never entered as a pilgrim. He said he is sensitive to the Invisible, the Transcendent, the Wholly-Other, but does not think of himself as a believer. Here was a beautiful "fish." We spoke at length about faith and God, and perhaps not enough about money. This is how it goes; I can't help being a pastor!

Then, before the main course, there was a presentation about the Cathedral, with video that showed the wear of time and the urgency of the work. I answered a few questions, then we began dessert, a *tarte tatin*—nothing out of the ordinary for a Frenchman, but in the land of fast food, a Norman element—washed down with a Veuve Clicquot champagne. The prospective patrons stayed until the end of the meal, which is a good sign, and they left with printed materials urging them to make a generous donation.

I said goodbye to the guests, thanked the consul general, and returned to my hotel. Now we would have to wait a few days to find out whether Notre Dame had touched their hearts.

The next day, my morning was free, and after a nice breakfast, I went out to discover the neighborhood—long and noisy streets, fire trucks, ambulances, police cars, traffic jams, drivers honking to let off steam but getting nowhere.

Then I was in Central Park, amidst joggers, dogs on their morning walks, and squirrels unafraid of the few tourists out at this time. Surrounded by all these skyscrapers that can make a person dizzy, I continued my journey by going to St. Patrick's, the "competing" cathedral. Some visitors were busy exploring the place; as for me, I prayed before the exposed relic of my patron saint. The French saints, Louis and the "little Thérèse," both have their own chapels there. Everything is white, perhaps too white; on the other hand, there is little noise because there are clearly fewer visitors than at Notre Dame.

In the afternoon I visited the leadership of the Metropolitan Museum of Art, the "American Louvre." We discussed the ways they raise money—$200 million per year to support the museum and its exhibitions! They have a team of forty employees for the work, so compared to them, we are small. We were looking for only 150 million euros for just a few years, and our team consisted of three people, plus a board that was a bit more constraining. But the development director graciously encouraged us—we've made a good start! Then it was time to visit the museum. What marvels, especially the exhibition on the liturgical vestments from the Vatican. Here again, my bias rears its head—at Notre Dame, we also have beautiful chasubles and copes that any cardinal of the holy church would dream of.

The American mentality is very open to requests for financial support. It's a part of the American tradition. So many foundations in New York! Ours became one more among them. But there is also the dimension of sharing: everyone is ready to name their major sponsors. Those who help support big projects in the United States are not kept hidden.

As we left *pedibus cum jambis*, I started to dream! I do love the Cathedral so much...and if we also cleaned the dirty chapels of the ambulatory...? And if...? I arrived back at the hotel full of hope.

The next day, the third day, I prepared to get back on the plane; I was already missing Notre Dame. I had to get back for the veneration of the Crown of Thorns, the diaconate ordinations, the knighting ceremony for the Knights of the Holy Sepulcher, the orthodox Vespers, and the imposition of the pallium on our Archbishop by the apostolic nuncio. A busy weekend that quickly made me forget about jet lag.

The next visit would probably be Washington. I am well aware of the efforts of my team to organize such meetings; they are hard workers, and I thank them for it.

11

OUR DISTINGUISHED GUESTS

ONE SUNDAY IN JULY, during the 10:00 a.m. Mass, I noticed an American delegation walking through Notre Dame. It was security people there to consider an official visit by the First Lady of the United States. Our communications officer was accompanying them discreetly, explaining the layout, while I celebrated the sacred liturgy. The officials departed without fanfare, though the armored car of the embassy was escorted by a police car.

On the evening of Tuesday, July 11, we received confirmation that Mrs. Trump would visit, accompanied by Mrs. Macron. It would happen on Thursday, at 4:00 p.m. On Wednesday, we ran through a "dress rehearsal" under high security. The leaders of both the French and American security teams asked me to walk through the exact course of the tour I would offer, without varying even a meter. With them, I marked out the steps we'd take to visit the chapel of the Pietà, listen to the organ, and venerate the Crown of Thorns. Many questions were discussed. Was it necessary to close Notre Dame during the visit? Was the rector going to speak English? Would he be accompanied by anyone else? And, if so, by whom? How long would the visit last? Would there be stairs?

After the rehearsal, I reviewed my notes and asked the Holy Spirit to touch the hearts of our guests during what would probably be a quick visit.

The next day was the big day. After the 11:30 a.m. Mass, we closed the Cathedral, and the explosive detection dogs arrived. These beautiful dogs rushed faster than the penitents in the confessionals. They made a respectful stop in front of each chapel while heavily armed security men climbed to the tribune. The French government had asked that the Cathedral remain open during the visit up to the middle of the nave. Once again, I showed the security people the route of the visit, and then we waited for the arrival of the two official entourages.

The rector was searched and the alarm squealed near his pocket—my rosary!

Brigitte Macron arrived but Melania Trump was still on her way. I was unable for the moment to approach our First Lady; I was placed at the foot of the steps of the sanctuary near the crowned Virgin and had to await the simultaneous entry of the two women.

At 4:00 p.m., the doors opened, the organ began to play, and the rector could finally approach to welcome them in the name of the cardinal-archbishop of Paris. The visit began with the statue of the Virgin of Paris, and to relax the atmosphere, I told the two First Ladies, "We begin the visit by greeting the First Lady of the world." And Melania, smiling, told me, "I like the Blessed Virgin." I was pleased—she would feel at home.

We continued the visit along the sanctuary and admired the representations of the risen Christ. I paused a few moments before the first appearance to Mary Magdalene and caught myself speaking Latin: "*Noli me tangere!*"—the words of the risen Christ to the holy woman when she wanted to hold on to him. Brigitte was impressed to hear the rector speak Latin, and I confided that I'm like a teacher of classical literature—we like to hear ourselves!

In front of the Pietà, I recalled the momentous events of our history that took place inside our Cathedral. Then we greeted the organist Yves Castagnet, while the great organ was played by one of our great titular organists, Olivier Latry. A moment of pure happiness. Then we contemplated the three rose windows, stopping at the south window that points our attention toward the kingdom!

Finally, it was time for the veneration of the Holy Crown, greatly anticipated by Mrs. Trump. I put on the red cope; it's always a solemn moment. Melania was very moved, so much so that Brigitte wished to venerate the holy relic as well.

The visit ended in front of the statue of the crowned Virgin; Melania lit two candles after depositing an offering in the box. Taking some time in silence and prayer, her eyes closed, Mrs. Trump remained standing. Meanwhile, Mrs. Macron signed the guestbook, then she was joined by the First Lady of the United States, who signed as well. The other half of the Cathedral was full of tourists and faithful, and our two distinguished guests greeted them from afar.

We did not go up to the tribune for lack of time and because of the high-heeled shoes both women were wearing. The official processions began to move; I accompanied them to the threshold of the Saint-Étienne portal. All in all, a relaxed and spiritual visit, just as I like them. After they left, many of the journalists present asked me about the visit. "What did Mrs. Trump say to the Virgin Mary?" they wondered. I told them, "That's a secret between the Mother of God and Melania." That's part of the mystery of the Cathedral.

One morning, I received a call from the vicar general asking me to host the secretary general of the Muslim World League, Mohammed al-Issa. The latter had been received the previous day by Pope Francis at the Vatican and had expressed his desire to visit our Cathedral. The security was less extensive, and I was able to welcome the official procession on the square in front of the central porch. Two large, white Mercedes escorted by motorcycle police officers arrived "discreetly." Saudi Arabian television was there to follow the visit. In full dress, accompanied by his entourage, the secretary general stood with me in the sanctuary, where I recalled the history of France and its connections with the Catholic faith.

From time to time, the journalists present asked us some questions. "What does it mean to you to receive the secretary general?" I said that I was happy to be able to continue the dialogue he'd had with the Holy Father. The secretary general talked about his own religion's tolerance and openness to other religions. I took the opportunity to talk about the conviction of our faith that each human person is created in the image and likeness of God and about the salvation won for all people without exception by Christ the only Savior. The interpreter translated my words. The visit lasted a good two hours, during which we had an enriching dialogue.

At the end of the visit, this distinguished visitor also signed the guestbook—an entire page where he expressed his gratitude in Arabic. The great door opened, and the secretary general advanced to his immaculate car, surrounded by the motorcycle escort. A cultural visit or interreligious dialogue? I don't know! But what I am sure of is that he was amazed by the beauty of Notre Dame.

I have also welcomed many ecclesiastical personalities, such as Cardinal Dominique Mamberti, the prefect of the Apostolic Signatura of the Roman Curia, and Cardinal Gérald Lacroix, the archbishop of Quebec and primate of Canada. These two cardinals have both presided over the Cathedral's festivities for the August 15 Solemnity of the Assumption of Mary.

The patriarch of Jerusalem. The sacristan of St. Peter's in Rome, happy to see this Cathedral so well maintained and so alive. Archbishop Mieczysław Mokrzycki of Lviv, who served as the deputy personal secretary of Pope John Paul II for seven years and of Pope Benedict XVI for two years. All, of course, ask to venerate the Holy Crown of Thorns.

Sometimes embassies request strictly cultural visits. In these cases, the rector organizes a visit to be led by a guide, but he does not show himself. This is the case for all Chinese officials. The Foreign Minister may not be photographed with the rector. The cultural aspect of the visit must be respected. On the other hand, the ambassador thanked me warmly for having made possible his artistic discovery of Notre Dame.

Each visit has its own flavor. When I received the Paris bar association, I tried to make an argument for the Christian roots of Europe. When I welcomed the prosecutor François Molins, accompanied by twenty European prosecutors specializing in terrorist cases, the visit was a bit informal because they needed to relax, but it was also marked by gravity and the gratitude of those representing Notre Dame Cathedral, which is such a target, but also so well protected.

Some guests come only to venerate the Crown. This was the case for Russia's Minister of Justice. Again, there was elevated security, including the closing of the Cathedral. Some Russian seminarians were there to sing litanies; the church was calm, and the bass voices resounded. The minister, on his knees, began to cry, and the veneration was prolonged because he took his time. Three times he asked to kiss the Crown. A beautiful testimony of faith. Upon leaving, he assured me that President Putin also wanted to visit Notre Dame to venerate this singular relic so dear to our Orthodox brethren.

Many national ambassadors, when they take up a new post in Paris, want to discover or rediscover Notre Dame—the ambassadors of the United States, Spain, Croatia, Belgium, Mexico, Great Britain, Australia, and Poland have all done so. The latter fell in love with the Cathedral and wished that one of our chapels might be dedicated to the famous Virgin of Częstochowa. But the chapel we had in mind needed to be restored first, and that would have been an expensive process. No problem! The Polish Senate, the Polish community of Paris, and a wealthy donor cooperated to create a beautiful setting for the Virgin of Jasna Góra. The Marshal of the Polish Senate inaugurated it with great fanfare in December 2017.

And then there are the military visitors. Some important visits are rather improvised, simply because we are warned only two hours before, for security reasons. One morning, I was informed that the Supreme Allied Commander of NATO would be arriving. I welcomed him and his family and his security team at the central doors. The visit went off without a hitch. Then I accompanied them as they prepared to leave and was surprised that there was no motorcade waiting. I learned that it was waiting for them elsewhere because the man's wife wanted to experience the Paris metro. Surrounded by eight guards, she was trying to stay simple, but one cannot always do what one wants.

It was a joy to introduce the chaplains of the German Federal Police to Notre Dame. Also to receive the chief of staff of the French military and his staff, with their wives, for an end-of-year visit that was supposed to be a surprise for the chief. I went all out for the occasion. It must be said that they all deserved it. On the roof of the Cathedral, between the two towers, we exchanged gifts around glasses of champagne. In short, France was there!

A more historical and political visit was with the students of the Institut des Hautes Etudes de Defense Nationale (IHEDN). The rector spoke of his role in the heart of the city, our relationship with the national and city governments, security issues, but also God!

Let's go back to politics: Paris city officials come to visit, one might say, their Cathedral. Many discover the artistic richness of this place; I take this opportunity to send a subtle message about our needs.

I meet regularly with the mayor of Paris, Anne Hidalgo. We get along well. She knows the importance of this place for the tourist life of her city. The Cathedral needs a welcome worthy of the name so that visitors can be comfortable to contemplate one of the masterpieces of the capital. Indeed, security concerns demand that we can't allow tourists who have suitcases or bulky bags. The Hôtel-Dieu, next to the Cathedral, was able to install a small luggage room, a shop, a sitting area, a suitable bathroom, and a room dedicated to the reception of groups, because the Cathedral does not have one. We must prepare for the 2024 Summer Olympic Games, which will be held in Paris. There are already twenty million people who visit the square each year. I dream of having a square like that of St. Peter's Basilica in Rome—where, by the way, there is no entry fee! Maintaining the French tradition of welcome is important to the mayor also. We sometimes go around the Cathedral to note the problems brought on by age and by pollution. Our common interest is our city of Paris; that's why there is a warm cooperation between us.

Large organizations also organize visits to the Cathedral as part of their conferences here in Paris. This is how I was able to meet the mathematician Cédric Villani, who was very touched by the Cathedral. He was surrounded by researchers who had spent two days at the Collège des Bernardins discussing the climate.

How can we not recall the Mass celebrated for the twenty-fifth anniversary of the death of King Baudoin of Belgium (1930–93), requested by his nieces from Spain? We included in our prayers his dear wife, Queen Fabiola (1928–2014). To tell the truth, they are surely already in the communion of the saints; the royal couple, in fact, offered an example for all those who assume a role of leadership. Allow me to share one of King Baudoin's many prayers:

Teach me, Jesus, to be for the people I meet what you want me to be: a witness to your love for humanity. But practically, Lord, in the particular place I occupy, what does that mean?

How should I go about it? Holy Spirit, do not leave me without your help, I beg you. Be my strength, my wisdom, my prudence, my humor, my courage, my dialectic.

O my God, forgive that this insect you made wishes to be a beautiful horse. Make me humble, almighty Lord, and happy to have been made small.

I think too often of the mission that You entrusted to me and for which I was born. I forget too often that I exist, before everything else for You, to adore You, to contemplate You, to love all those You put in my path, but to love them as You love them and with Your love.

This is holiness in action.

There are so many other visits we could mention, such as that of the Prime Minister of Israel, Benjamin Netanyahu; a Gabonese minister; the First Lady of Panama; the Polish Minister of Foreign Affairs; the Georgian delegation to UNESCO; and the Ambassador of the Ivory Coast to UNESCO, accompanied by his son to give thanks for having received a baccalaureate.

I will end with the police chief, my friend across town. We have good relations; his office's security keeps an eye on me. Very attentive to the life of the Cathedral, he receives the Cathedral's pastoral program each week in order to review it with an eye toward our protection. His staff is regularly invited to our concerts, as is the commissioner of the 4th district. They sometimes run into Mr. Delanoë, the retired mayor of Paris who likes to return to his Cathedral to listen to the choir because he misses it. Obviously, I also keep in touch with Philippe Bélaval, president of the Office of National Monuments. It's a strong political friendship, with each of us guarding our territory.

One of the more recent visits, as I write this, was that of the newly appointed U.S. Ambassador, Jamie McCourt. With a bit less of an entourage than Melania Trump, she arrived in her armored car, along with a police escort. Mrs. McCourt is fluent in our language because she studied at the Sorbonne when she was young, and she already knew the Cathedral well. She thanked me for the special Franco-American friendship, and we shared some conversation about French society, the political climate, the situation of religions, and more. We completed our visit on the roof of the sacristy, where we have some beehives; the ambassador appreciated our honey!

These visits reinforce our ties with the United States. I am also invited to the U.S. embassy for the New Year's celebration and the Independence Day celebration. It was on one such occasion that I met the popular French singer and actress Line Renaud, sitting in a corner of the lounge before going down to the park. I approached her to introduce myself, and she gave me a warm hug. She said she remembered me well from the last time she'd been at Notre Dame for an episcopal ordination; she was seated next to the television personality Jacques Martin. During the procession of offerings, African women carried baskets of fruit, and Line, turning to her neighbor, asked him why such a procession. "Because Jean-Michel is from Marseille," replied Mr. Martin. That day, at the embassy, I invited her to rediscover the Cathedral on the occasion of her eighty-first birthday.

We always must be ready to welcome a special guest! One Sunday morning in October, the security of the president of Chile let us know he would be present at the 11:30 a.m. Mass. We had only twenty minutes to reserve the first two rows and to place the necessary chair for our unexpected guest. I welcomed

Mr. Sebastián Piñera and his wife, accompanied by the delegation and their bodyguards, at the central portal. The president, during his official trip to Paris, had wished to participate in the Mass to entrust his country to Our Lady. This is the diplomatic role of the Mother of God—to put peace in our hearts.

On another occasion, a telephone call from the Ministry of the Interior came at 2:00 p.m.: "The American senator Orrin Hatch will come to visit the Cathedral at 4:00 p.m." The rector had to adjust to this development on the fly. Suddenly I was ready to welcome the official entourage. Senator Hatch walked through the nave with an authoritative step. He was amazed by the Cathedral and paid close attention to my explanations. The visit concluded on the square. He kissed me, saying, "I love you"—in front of his wife, thank God.

For the commemorations marking the centenary of the end of World War I, we decorated the Cathedral as it was in 1918. It was superb. The president of Romania and his wife came to Friday Vespers to see their flag and to entrust their country to the Virgin. As they do every year for November 11, representatives of the British Commonwealth came to commemorate the victory. I sang "La Marseillaise" and "God Save the Queen," and the chaplains were surprised to hear me sing in English. Then for the evening Mass presided over by our archbishop, we rang the bells in honor of the dead. The French Republican Guard was as moved as the rest of us, and the minute of silence was prolonged. Time to come back down to earth.

12

THE ADVENTURE OF SOUND AND LIGHT

Dame de Coeur

SOON AFTER MY ARRIVAL at Notre Dame, I met with the Catholic media consultant Arnaud Bouthéon, who shared with me his desire to project a stunning sound and light show on the facade of Notre Dame. Like me, he wanted to restore the vibrance of crowds and the faithful to the Cathedral's square, since these had notably decreased in recent years in reaction to fears of terrorism.

What he had in mind was a spiritual and missionary spectacle that, like the mystery plays of the Middle Ages, would be a true catechesis. I met with Bruno Sellier, the creator of another such show, *A Night at Les Invalides*, and explained to him what I envisioned: "To see the Cathedral in all its splendor to the sound of the great organ, to turn people's eyes towards Our Lady, and to help them rediscover Notre Dame." In the third millennium, we need to rediscover the tenderness of God. Mary, the Mother of God, is undoubtedly a privileged way. A "Queen of Hearts" she is!

The story told in *Dame de Coeur* opens in 1917, when the U.S. military arrived at the end of World War I. A French nurse is caring for a badly wounded soldier, and she asks him what his last wish would be. To see Notre Dame Cathedral, he says. His dream comes true, and he discovers a Cathedral of light. This nurse is also the queen of hearts.

Because the sound and light show required an investment of five hundred thousand euros, we started looking for sponsors. We didn't want to charge spectators any kind of fee. The adventure began by turning to the Supreme Knight of the Knights of Columbus, Carl Anderson, who was interested in our project and ready to help financially.

So in August 2017, I traveled to the Knights of Columbus convention in St. Louis in the United States. It was a privileged moment that allowed me to discover the work of the Knights. I also made a pilgrimage to St. Louis Cathedral, which holds a relic of the holy king's tunic that Cardinal François Marty, the archbishop of Paris in the mid-twentieth century, had given to the archbishop of this archdiocese. The Cathedral's frescoes depict St. Louis holding the Crown of Thorns in his hands. Like so many American cities, the streets are wide and the buildings are very tall. I was welcomed at the convention like a king. Cardinals and many bishops from around the world were present.

But who are the Knights? An Irish priest, moved with compassion at the poverty of his immigrant brothers and sisters in the United States, created this Catholic association in the service of the church. The organization, whose members are all men, offers a life insurance program that protects families. Some of the profits are used to help the poor. Today, there are more than a million Knights around the world, and the group comes to the aid of people affected by earthquakes and hunger. Unlike the French, who do not like to talk about their finances, American organizations typically publicize their profits with great transparency.

I admired their charity in action. The finances are not complex, since the money is at the service of the poor and parishes.

The Knights of Columbus are present in many French parishes and help in the mission of evangelization, setting up events and taking on material tasks to lighten the priest's agenda. Members meet in groups to deepen their faith and spirituality. The presence of so many bishops and priests among its ranks underlines the group's unwavering commitment to the church.

Being an early bird, despite the jet lag, I went down to the hotel restaurant to have breakfast. I discovered a big buffet and bottles of ketchup on the tables. A man in a yellow T-shirt and shorts, who was already seated, called to me. I approached and introduced myself. He squeezed my shoulder warmly and said, "I'm the archbishop of New York." He seemed more like a cowboy to me than a red-cassocked prelate. But he also knows how to wear the red cassock, and he wears it well. I thought of Pope Francis, who invites us to closeness with others.

Meeting him made me recall meeting a previous archbishop of New York, Cardinal John O'Connor. The occasion was the 1997 World Youth Day, which was held in Paris, and I was rector of Sacred Heart Basilica at the time. We welcomed a large group of Americans to the Basilica, led by Cardinal O'Connor. Over seventy-five years old at the time, he presided over a remarkable three hours with three thousand young people, making them laugh, but also getting them on their knees to worship the Lord present in the Eucharist. Afterward, we found ourselves socializing in the room set aside for the bishops. Cardinal O'Connor was drinking a double scotch—he was a former military chaplain, and he knew how to lift his elbow! It was announced that the pope (at that time, John Paul II) had just landed, and so it was time to leave Sacred Heart. But the cardinal knew that in the next room was a group of disabled people waiting to take a picture with him. His secretary pressed him a little, and he replied, "The pope will wait; I want to spend some time with these young people." What a beautiful image of pastoral closeness!

The Knights convention was the occasion of magnificent meetings with pastors from all over the world. Accompanied by a young priest who served as my interpreter, it was my first contact with the American church—which knows how to throw a party!

Welcomed by the Supreme Knight, I was able to share with the members the situation of the church in France. The Knights count on us; we are the eldest daughter of the church. Pope Francis says that we are "the grandmother," but a grandmother who has the mission to encourage her granddaughters!

When the convention concluded, I returned to Paris to prepare the festivities for the Feast of the Assumption, which always draw many faithful to Notre Dame. On the evening before the feast, we first hosted a concert of Gregorian chant performed by the choir, then a great Mass presided by a guest archbishop, followed by a spiritual vigil that ended with the traditional torchlight procession around the Cathedral. It is always a beautiful and prayerful event. And then on the feast day, we made the traditional procession that traverses the two islands in the Seine river, the Île de la Cité and the Île Saint-Louis. A huge crowd participated, with the rector in the lead.

In September, advertising for the *Dame de Coeur* show began, and reservations began pouring in quickly. The team began to grow. We had to recruit volunteers for welcoming, security, and the distribution of the booklets. The technical team made many requests, starting with one to turn off the lights of the square. On the night before, we set up for the show and went through a rehearsal at midnight.

Finally, D-Day—or perhaps we should say, N-Night—arrived. The first show was reserved for the two thousand special guests. What splendor! What a magnificent show—the Cathedral lit up in multicolored lights! Victor Hugo would have been thrilled! The facade of Notre Dame took on a mysterious dimension, and all the spectators became pilgrims going to Mary, who was waiting for them. My dream was coming true—this crowd of eighty thousand people over those five nights drew near to the Pietà.

On the first evening, I welcomed former French President Giscard d'Estaing and his wife; the mayor of Paris Anne Hidalgo; the French politician Valérie Pécresse; many ambassadors; and future supporters of the restoration of our spire and chevet. An official dinner was held at the end of the show in the mansion that belongs to the City of Paris and that was lent to us for the occasion, and the great chef Alain Ducasse prepared a real banquet. I won't be coy: we saw the special guests as potential donors, and this was also an effort at fundraising. Chef Ducasse donated his work for the evening; it was his way of participating in the much-needed project. The Cathedral and great cuisine go well together!

Two shows were presented each evening: the first at 7:30, in a rather family-oriented atmosphere, and the other at 9:00, which attracted many young people. We did not expect so many people, and the prefecture forced us for the last shows to post security guards. It's not always easy to manage a crowd of more than ten thousand people on a public square.

One of the chaplains and I stood at Rue du Cloître to greet the pilgrims. So many outstretched hands, faces known and unknown, Parisians who discovered the soul of the Cathedral! The spectators were so awestruck and moved that many forgot to provide a donation at the locations provided at the exits as they left—just a small mistake, but a costly one. But what could be done? Especially if it brings them back to Notre Dame as pilgrims! The press was unanimous in its praise for the show, and parts of it were broadcast in media throughout the world, even in China!

While we did not cover all the expenses through donations, the missionary dimension was a real success. Following the show, we saw increases in the numbers of people coming to the Cathedral for our liturgies, spiritual reflections, Vespers, and multiple processions on the square. Is this a coincidence? If so, then it's a divine one. We have little impact on tourism; on the other hand, pilgrims will come back if we meet their needs.

We had the show again the following year, and two hundred thousand people came! This time, donations covered the expenses and even part of the deficit from the previous year. God is good!

What a blessed place the square is, in its own way, preparing people's hearts for a possible encounter with the Lord inside his Cathedral. That's why, from the time I arrived, I became interested in this part of Notre Dame, an integral part of the building. The preambles to faith can be experienced in front of the facade. True beauty, true catechesis, if one manages to "read" the facade. The Invisible becomes present to each visitor.

I have always thought that this Cathedral is a privileged place for the action of God.

I have always thought that this Cathedral is a place of transmission of faith.

I have always thought it is a spiritual landmark. It is one of the spiritual lungs of Paris, the other being Sacré-Coeur. What a grace for a priest to have the experience of being rector of both of these two places! On one hand, the heart of Christ; on the other, that of Mary.

Part Three

THE FUTURE OF THE CATHEDRAL

13

EVANGELIZATION AT NOTRE DAME

HAVING DESCRIBED THE rector's work and life, I'd like to turn now to the future of the Cathedral, even if that belongs ultimately to God. The present calls to the future. Thus, I wish to share with you my convictions, my way of living my priesthood through the teaching of Pope Francis, and my love of the church. My first two years at Notre Dame helped me understand the building's needs. From this experience, I needed to reflect, with all my collaborators, priests and laity, on the pastoral priorities that needed to be strengthened or put in place.

As I have already written, the liturgy is the source and summit of the life of this spiritual place. The rest of our pastoral ministry is founded on that. We must always attend to the liturgy because the faithful, especially those just passing through, come first to encounter the Lord.

In our time, the church has rediscovered the evangelizing power of the liturgy. "If you want to know what we believe," said St. Augustine, "listen to what we sing." The liturgy evangelizes people, whose earthly lives have meaning only if they are open to heaven. As St. Paul VI wrote in his apostolic exhortation *Evangelii Nuntiandi*,

> The fatigue produced these days by so much empty talk and the relevance of many other forms of communication must not however diminish the permanent power of the word, or cause a loss of confidence in it. The word remains ever relevant, especially when it is the bearer of the power of God. This is why St. Paul's axiom, "Faith comes from what is heard," also retains its relevance: it is the Word that is heard which leads to belief. (no. 42)[1]

Pilgrims come to the Cathedral to see its beauty, but they also want a spiritual experience. Hence the importance of hospitality, the possibility of celebrating at the Pietà or the main altar, the catechetical reflections on the grace of God. Why do they come to Notre Dame? To confide in Mary, to discover the mystery of salvation through the Crown of Thorns, to be reconciled to God through the sacrament of confession. It seems to me that the grace of this place is the conversion of hearts: "Holy Mary, Mother of God, pray for us sinners." She draws them here to show them the tenderness of the Father. The chaplains are daily witnesses to this. What wounds, what suffering is presented to Christ, thanks to his Mother! But is not this the role of the mother church?

Many tourists enter the Cathedral. Some are Christians who hesitate to enter because it has been so long since they have stepped into a church. Others want to be indifferent, but do they come out untouched by the place? Others are believers of different religions—what does it matter? The Cathedral is a place of rest for one's spirit. Muslim tourists come to pray to Mary and sometimes talk to a priest to understand things like the mystery of the Holy Trinity. Finally, there are tourists who are not believers but are open to transcendence. And there are also those who are hostile to faith, who don't enter but instead remain outside on the square. But Our Lady is there, too! All of us are seekers of God until the time we will see God face-to-face.

Because of all these people, the desire to share our faith increases and evangelization is a priority. It is true that for many, this word is synonymous with proselytism. We are sometimes paralyzed by the word *tolerance* or expressions like "All religions are equal, everyone is beautiful, everyone is nice, everyone is saved." Yes, but saved by whom? How? From what? Let's pause, then, to reflect on evangelization at Notre Dame.

First, what does it mean to evangelize?

Evangelization is not a call to awaken or reawaken this pagan or sleepy world, but a call to return to the living sources of the gospel. This is what Jesus did by proclaiming the good news of the coming of God into this world. It is also true that Christ is the evangelizer of humanity. He announces salvation to us all—and he not only promises it but gives it. Through him, the bridge is established between heaven and earth; Passover is fulfilled in the person of Christ, who descended from heaven to earth in order to bring us, the children of God, back to the house of the Father of heaven. This is the true gospel of God that gives us true salvation, the source of true peace because it is a gift of eternal life. This is the great and good news to be proclaimed on the square and in the Cathedral. The imperative of his announcement lies in the incomparable richness of this hope! The call to evangelize is based on the example of Christ, which concludes in all four Gospels with sending his disciples on mission. How can we not respond again and again to this word of the Lord, a response that every generation must proclaim with renewed urgency because "the love of Christ urges us on" (2 Cor 5:14)?

We must tirelessly repeat the words of St. Paul the Apostle to the nations: "If I proclaim the gospel, this gives me no ground for boasting, for an obligation is laid on me, and woe to me if I do not proclaim the gospel!" (1 Cor 9:16). And then he adds, proudly and humbly, "I am entrusted with a commission" (1 Cor 9:17).

From this requirement to spread the gospel, no disciple of Christ is dispensed. Was it not a woman, a forgiven sinner, whom Jesus chose to make "the Apostle to the Apostles," showing us that each baptized person must be a witness of his resurrection?

Not only is evangelization part of the life of the church, but we can also say with Vatican II and St. Paul VI's *Evangelii Nuntiandi* that the church is made to evangelize. Its nature and purpose are missionary. If evangelization is constitutive of the life of the church, it is incarnated today only by taking into account the spiritual, social, and cultural context in which the church exists. It is for this that we bring to the modern world the vivifying and permanent power of the mystery of Christ. Before a world that discovers the ever-greater proportions of the cosmos, human history, and life in society, we have to expand in ourselves the awareness of the mission of the church and to offer the vision of salvation in all its cosmic magnitude—the greatness of Christ handing over the kingdom to the Father at the end of time fuels our spirits.

Our younger generations see the magnitude of the mission that awaits them today. They need to see the difficulties clearly so that they might redouble their hope and enthusiasm. They must bear witness to the hope and joy of the risen Christ. The Synod on Young People, the Faith, and Vocational Discernment, held at the Vatican in 2018, addressed these concerns. This means that the time for heroic mission is not over—on the contrary! It will unfold with an unknown scale, calling for self-denial and greater service than ever. Young people know that Christians can no longer limit their horizons to the immediate environment, to their relatives; they are bound, in the truth of their love, to bear their message to all people, especially the poor. Evangelization integrates the fact that the church has developed a new awareness of its missionary identity and addresses a world that has undergone considerable economic, cultural, and social upheaval.

We have spoken in recent years of a "new evangelization," but in what way is this evangelization called new, because is it not, by definition, always new? The world today experiences such constant changes that there are always situations emerging around us that we can incessantly call new.

When the march of the world accelerates, the gospel of salvation must step up its pace! When the conflicts of this world intensify, the gospel of peace must run to meet them. In a world that forgets the very name of the Creator, the gospel of God must make his voice heard. When our world threatens to sink into idolatry, the gospel of the kingdom can only stand in its way to say, "You fool! This very night your life is being demanded of you. And the things you have prepared, whose will they be?" (Luke 12:20).

But the world of yesterday also experienced changes, developments, upheavals, renewal of structures, and revolutions in mentalities. And each time, it is the Spirit who renews the face of the earth. Let us think of Origen and St. Athanasius in the Hellenistic world; St. Ambrose and St. Augustine in the Roman world; St. Leo or St. Gregory the Great in the face of the invasion of the barbarians; St. Bernard, St. Thomas, and St. Francis during the Middle Ages; St. Ignatius of Loyola and St. Vincent de Paul in the aftermath of the Reformation and the Renaissance. We can see how the gospel renews itself constantly. It's up to us to adopt the apostolic and creative daring of these saints.

We need to take better stock of the weakening of faith and the atheism of our society. The church faces the challenges of nonbelief and religious indifference. We see new spiritualities around a god without a face, disconnected from history. At the same time, beauty seems never to have been more sought after, including as a way of evangelization. This is why Notre Dame is a privileged place and we must highlight the beauty of the place.

Fifty years ago, the church in the West was still living in a Christian context. The symbols, the representations, the social behaviors, the whole of our culture were bathed in Christianity. But today, Christian referents that used to be common are now doubted or unknown. We see it all the time among visitors to the Cathedral. The "language of the tribe" is no longer understood and has not been transmitted. Christian anthropology is no longer a shared understanding; we see this in bioethics, for example, or education.

Evangelization must therefore unfold in a new paradigm, that of "postmodernity." We cannot close our eyes! Our pluralistic society proposes other means of fulfillment than Christ. For many of our contemporaries, Christianity is one opinion among many, which is understood, at best, as merely one of the possible ways to happiness. There is a syncretistic relativization of the truth.

So how do we approach this relativism? By personal testimony. Our lives must demonstrate the relevance of the gospel and attest to how God can transform us. Faith brings something decisive, something that exceeds the material, spiritual comfort into which I can settle. Let's not be "parked Christians" who are standing still and thinking that they have already arrived at the goal. Faith allows us to take a step back and strengthen our inner being.

Evangelization often starts with a testimony. The first testimony is that of Christ, relayed and taken up by that of the apostles. This is about being able to give account for our reasons to believe and hope. But note: It is Christ who gives faith! We are only instruments. But where to give this testimony of ours? In the public square. We need "missionaries of the square." These are the preambles to faith of which I have already spoken. We must prepare people's hearts so that their visit to Notre Dame can bear fruit.

Faith is a begetting. It is not a question of reducing evangelization to the transmission of a certain set of truths. It's about bringing a new world to life. Without dogmatism.

The messenger and the message must coincide. Christianity is not primarily a set of moral rules, wise words, or a spirituality—it is *Someone*, the Christ. Mary gave birth to a child, not to an ideology or to a Bible! Christianity is part of history. It takes shape in the history of humanity, in the life of a people, Israel, in the earthly trajectory of a man, Jesus, who takes up my own history.

Because life is hard, our contemporaries are looking for something. Christianity proposes an answer that is not a flight out of oneself, but the discovery within oneself and within our world of a presence—the presence of God. It seems to me that Notre Dame can foster this spiritual experience. We strive to help the faithful make such a discovery through the spiritual programs we offer.

The genius of Christianity is the mystery of the incarnation. God is near. The great God has become small. This descent of God by his Son, even into suffering and death, expresses his infinite love. So I do not have to be afraid of God or seek ersatz happiness in artificial paradises. I must discover in myself the presence of the One who makes me worthy of who I am, who makes my life good and even extraordinary, and who offers me the way to salvation.

Today, we are experiencing the enormous influence of social media, the content of which is often far from the values advocated by the gospel. The media world is not just indifferent; it can be hostile. Faith and morality are affected. Christian values are attacked, mocked. "Because you do not belong to the world...the world hates you" (John 15:19).

In this context, invaded by so many human words, our challenge is to give the word back to God so that humanity can hear again the word of God. "Faith comes from what is heard" (Rom 10:17). The challenge for the church is to find an instrument, an appropriate medium. Above the cacophony of voices, the word of God does not have to fear, because it is of another order.

Our world is a world of entertainment. This is not new. But entertainment has become omnipresent, and all the sparkles of technological and technical novelty shimmer before our eyes.

The gospel announces joy and peace, but it also proclaims the Beatitudes, the call to renunciation, the demands of love and justice, of service. It is not "fun"! How can we make it heard in a world that always wants to be entertained? What is the strategy?

The time of scientism is over. The great philosophical utopias and reference systems have disappeared. We are in a time of economic globalization, individualistic withdrawal, and the awakening of superstitions in the supermarket of beliefs. We surf along happily on the emotional surface, seeking only "to be comfortable in our skin." Parishes, places of pilgrimage, and works of solidarity are missionary places where the church offers "the service of transcendence and understanding of what is ultimate." It insists upon the sacred value of the dignity of every human person.

But it is our personal lives that constitute the primary means of evangelization. While the church is so often put on trial, all of us who are Christian must evangelize through the way we live, so that our lives in society, among our families, and at work will always demonstrate our commitment to Christ and his church. We evangelize ourselves by evangelizing. This means that we must go back to basics. The lived authenticity of the proclaimed message is what is most essential.

May the Cathedral and its community of leaders and believers, like each one of us, be for the world a house of God, the body of Christ, and a temple of the Spirit. May it be a communion of love, that love may shine from it. May it offer truth, that people will hear it. May it be humble, that it will touch people. May it be poor, that it will be pleasing to people. May it be chaste, that it will engage people's interest. May it be obedient to the gospel, that it will surprise and attract people. May it be merciful, that people will forgive it for not being perfect. May it live in a joyful hope and a foolproof faith, that people will seek its secret and its path.

The church still needs to be re-evangelized! There is still mediocrity, lukewarmness, and even unacceptable scandals.

We must live like children of light. It is through the love we live that the God of love will be proclaimed. It is through the holiness lived from the depths of our hearts that the glory of the thrice-holy God will be revealed.

The church does not have to disengage from the world, but to free itself from it. We needn't cut ourselves off from the world, but we need to be wary of it. The teaching of Pope Francis is clear: We must avoid worldliness.

Evangelization at the heart of the church requires a new attitude of simplicity, authenticity of heart, goodness of life, and humility pushed to our limits. Let us listen to Pope Francis:

> The characteristic of the missionary's style is, so to speak, a *face*, which consists in the *poverty of means*. His accoutrement responds to a criterion of modesty....The Teacher wants them to be free and unhampered, without reserves and without favors, certain only of the love of the One who sends them.[2]

May the church live in charity that becomes mercy and tenderness. I love the way the philosopher Henri Bergson put it: "Saints do not need to be heard. Their very existence is a call."

14

OUR METHODS OF EVANGELIZATION

SO, HOW TO GO about it then? I'll mention some methods of evangelization specific to the Cathedral.

First, we have an active presence in the digital world. Our website is visited daily by about 11,000 people, and we receive thousands of e-mails. We are also present on social media, with nearly 350,000 people following us on Facebook, 15,000 on Twitter, and 18,000 on Instagram.

We maintain a strong presence in the media world, to help us reach out to people, to speak in the public square, as Jesus did and as his apostles did after him. The airwaves—Radio Notre Dame, Masses broadcast on France Culture, and the Lenten sermons—are essential. The Catholic cable station KTO and the televised Mass expand the size of the Cathedral. Many of the faithful watch our services on KTO. We receive letters with beautiful testimonies. When I go out to speak somewhere or when I go on vacation, sometimes I hear, "I've seen you on KTO!" When I had to have some surgery on my hand recently, while I was on the operating table, a kind scrub nurse approached me to say, "You don't know me, but I see you every evening on KTO." Established by Cardinal Lustiger in 1999, KTO is a way to reach isolated Christians and enable them to be part of the life of our Cathedral.

Our communications director is in regular contact with the secular media, and I rarely refuse requests for information or interviews related to Notre Dame. Giving testimony of what we do here expands awareness of the Cathedral in society. Art and culture can become, more than ever, openings to faith. Put at the service of the gospel, the media can help us extend the reach of the word of God, and through them we can bring the good news to millions of people. It is always a joy to meet journalists and the audio and video technicians who work with them.

One project we worked on recently was recorded in 3D. I was astonished to find myself in front of a spherical camera with two eyes, fixed on a tripod, with the journalist hidden behind a curtain. As we shot a sequence in the sacristy, the journalist was under the table, while "the ball" moved comfortably around. What a world! That evening, after returning to my room, I reread Georges Bernanos's *Tradition of Freedom* and found the question he posed, which I already cited above: "Has the Machine World made men better? Has it made him more humane?"[1] And a little further on:

> The Machine Civilization has its motto: "Technique first! Technique everywhere!" Fools! You fancy that technique will do no more, at the worst, than direct your material activities, and since you are expecting a "five hour week" tomorrow, with the Fun Fairs pen day and night, the possibility does not disturb you greatly....The Technical State will have no enemy, tomorrow, but the "man who is not like other men," or again, "the man who has time to waste," or, more simply: "the man who does not believe in Technique."[2]

Those lines were written in 1945 by St. Bernanos, prophet of our time! What I am talking about here is obviously not a matter of being against machines, robots, or virtual intelligence, but of making sure that technology is always at the service of humanity, and not the other way around.

Another priority is the ecumenism that the Crown of Thorns helps us foster. Advancing along this path is important. Much progress has already been made in relations between Jews and Christians and between the churches of the Reformation and the church of Rome. This journey continues also between the Orthodox church and Catholicism. Faced with the rise of a militant atheism or an ambient secularization, Christians must come ever closer to one another and give a witness of unity. Jesus prayed "that they may all be one" (John 17:21). Unity is possible, and thanks especially to the presence of the Crown of Thorns, which is a treasure for all Christians, the Cathedral must be an artisan of that unity.

Notre Dame is a spiritual landmark. I am convinced that in every diocese there is some sanctuary, however small, which, by its location, its history, its beauty, its cultural and spiritual impact, attracts people. It is like a lighthouse. It calls people together. Today, we have rediscovered the value of pilgrimage; people like such gatherings. The spiritual can go hand in hand with the cultural. It is also an expression of popular piety.

I often say, based on my experience at both Sacred Heart and Notre Dame, that our sanctuaries are "flagship" places—places where Christians who feel outside the community can come back to the church, where tourists become pilgrims, and where pilgrims find rest along the journey.

Popular piety, too long neglected, invites us to imitate the creative spirituality of our forebears in faith. Let's face it, it was fashionable a few years ago to dismiss it. It was cast out of pastoral ministry, with the predicable result of marginalizing many of the faithful who were attached to such piety. We sought to emphasize a more intellectual understanding of one's faith, forgetting the importance of the understanding of the heart. Since then, we have seen the return of processions, pilgrimages, and devotions that we had neglected, that many young people now embrace. I believe that we must give a prominent place to this popular piety, while using sound discernment. I'll share with you some criteria.

How does this popular piety help one to enter the mystery of God? A more affective approach must not be rejected; the mystery of the incarnation is no small thing! But excess distracts us from the mystery.

"Father, what a wonderful prayer—I felt chills!" This is not the purpose of prayer. If you have chills, take aspirin because you probably have a fever. Such popular piety can become idolatrous. We know the risks. It's up to us to transform these practices from idol to icon. This calls for catechesis that is both patient and filled with charity. We also know the risk of division, especially when diverse cultures and their traditions are involved. Sound ecclesial criteria are essential. A path of purification can help us rediscover the distinctiveness of our faith. The faithful sometimes engage in forms of syncretism, with rites borrowed from different religions. Again, we must evangelize these rites. There is a whole work of inculturation. It is a matter of entering and helping others to enter into the obedience of faith and at the same time being docile to the action of the Holy Spirit. We must embrace the tension between faithfulness and creativity. As St. Vincent de Lérins said, "Say things in a new way without saying new things."

Popular piety does not belong to the past. It is a very present reality that is part of the soul of our Cathedral. That's why I have introduced more processions on our square. We pray with our feet as well as our hearts and minds. For the same reason, I reestablished pilgrimages.

We have seen the church in recent decades seek to rid itself of triumphalism, to be present at the level of the real lives of people. This has invited some secularization. As a result, the church has no doubt gained simplicity, authenticity, and humility. But it has lost some apostolic effectiveness.

A new evangelization has in any case become necessary. It can only happen through a return to true clarity, not just in appearance, but in truth. Our world expects the church to speak of its faith clearly and firmly, not to simply "try" to proclaim, but to proclaim.

Families are also privileged places of evangelization. St. John Paul II reminded us of this throughout his pontificate. Evangelization happens within the domestic church. Transformed by the gospel, the family offers to the world the truth it has received. As we know, our society is in a deep crisis due to a failure to transmit values. No doubt it is necessary to heal the culture. Family prayer and participation in liturgical life are important ways of doing this. It is within the family that faith is transmitted.

There is no need to embrace whatever is most in fashion on any given day. Our young people need landmarks. It is important to listen to them, but it is equally important to lead them and show them the way. It is not easy! I'm not saying that we alone hold the truth, but what I'm sure of is that Christ is the Redeemer of humanity and that he offers us the model of what it means to be a free human person. We must rediscover this Christian anthropology: What is the human person? A being created in the image and likeness of God.

Christian education consists in forming free persons. To educate is to awaken and form the life of the spirit, that is, the courage of conscience, the freedom of knowledge, and the strength to love. Our young people need to understand the heritage that gives them life, that gives meaning to their present and impetus to their growth. The family is therefore a kind of challenge to a society focused only on the ephemeral, the immediately consumable, disposable goods, signs, and words. The mission of parents is to open the hearts of their children to what is possible. This is the way of freedom. To be free doesn't mean that everything is possible, but that one knows what is possible. The Cathedral, as the mother church, must be able to accommodate its children and therefore all their families.

The new generations are full of new hope that the church must help them sustain. Young people are only seeking a frank openness and a true challenge. They do not want to be old-fashioned, but they don't want to be lulled into mediocrity either. This world needs new Don Boscos, true educators. The future of the gospel is for those who love life, this life that is true just as it is eternal.

The time has come to rediscover and adopt a way of communicating that reiterates the beauty of the gospel message, the relevance of the good news, the greatness of this ideal of life, truth, and love. Following the great theologian saints, we must stand up for the truth. It is not easy! But we must do it.

How do the rector and the chaplains—as well as everyone else who works at Notre Dame—carry out this evangelization? "Underlying [their] missionary dynamism was the holiness of the first Christians and the first communities."[3]

To respond to the demands of mission today, it is not enough to renew pastoral methods, nor to better organize and coordinate the forces of the church, nor even to explore with more acumen the biblical and theological foundations of faith. Rather, a new momentum for holiness must be created among missionaries and throughout the Christian community. This means that the church not only needs more missionaries, but missionaries with a deep spirituality. This is why we must live in communion with the mystery of Christ.

The apostle is swept up by Jesus. At the origin of his or her apostolic life is Jesus who calls and sends. The apostle is not primarily one who teaches a doctrine or speaks truths or offers some service—the apostle's mission is to introduce a *person*, in order to invite and help others to enter into intimate communion with him.

It is an intimate relationship, born of an experience of faith, that knows that Christ is sent by the Father as the only savior of the world. Rooted in this faith, the apostle is a person of the beatitudes, a person of joy, a person of hope. The apostle's life is constantly animated by the great desire to share with others the experience of Christ.

Many people, especially in the rich nations, are indifferent or hostile to this experience, interested only in material things. But sometimes these things provoke in us a weariness, a hopelessness.

We must not forget all those who seek Christ and his gospel. We must start from this act of hope: humanity needs Jesus Christ. This is why we must have a great familiarity with Christ and with his gospel. We must allow ourselves to be transformed by the gospel. We must transform our mentality, our way of living, our criteria of judgment, our values. We cannot witness to Christ if we do not reflect his image. And this is why silence and contemplation are so important. Silence, the ability to listen and wonder in order to be swept up by Christ. Contemplation, in order to live this intimacy; it is this contemplation that grounds this ever deeper personal relationship with Christ. It is about allowing oneself to be penetrated by the mystery of Christ, at all levels—mentality, thoughts, standards, judgments, feelings, motivations, choice of activities.

To live the spirituality of Christ, sent by the Father, means allowing ourselves to be formed in his image. Indeed, Christ let himself be seized by the Father's plan, to do only the Father's will. He renounced himself, gave himself up, in order to be totally free for the gospel. Such interior freedom must constantly grow in us. We are prisoners of our world. But it is not a matter of escaping from our world, but of recognizing what holds us back, our resistance that prevents us from evangelizing. It is a question of living in complete docility to the Spirit, because it is the Spirit who shapes the disciple's heart and mind, bringing us more and more in conformity with Christ, in order to understand his mystery and to follow him. It is the Spirit who makes us courageous witnesses of Christ. This docility is necessary because the mission is difficult. If we let ourselves be guided by the Spirit, we will have the courage to proclaim the gospel with frankness and wisdom.

That's the lifestyle of any evangelizer. We know it is not easy to live according to this inner voice nor to always understand it, because discernment is needed. Our own interests, passions, selfishness, and sinfulness can get in the way. This is why the disciple's simplicity is so important—to free him from all passions and selfish interests, be they material, intellectual, or ideological. We are then called to live this transition from a life centered on oneself to a life centered on Christ. Only the apostle who is willing to die to herself will be able to listen to the voice of the Holy Spirit. She will also work with others, respecting past and present evangelistic work. Mission is never a purely individual commitment; it is the work of the whole church, a specifically ecclesial act.

15

THE PRIORITIES OF MISSION

NO DOUBT FORMED by my reading of St. Thérèse of Lisieux, I think the *first priority* is to discover the true face of God.

We must start with all the false representations of God that are the fruit of an undigested Jansenism! It must be said that we don't have a good grasp of the Old Testament and that we are infected by Marcionism. For the second-century heretic Marcion, the God of the Old Testament was not the same as the God of the New Testament. The Old Testament God is severe and hard, while the New Testament God is a Father full of tenderness. But it's the same God!

The Name of God, "I AM WHO I AM" (Exod 3:14), could make God seem distant and inaccessible. The holiness of God opens an abyss that is unbridgeable to any creature.

"Holy One of God" (John 6:69) is perhaps the oldest title given to Christ to express the mysterious beyond that radiated from his person. Holiness manifests itself with brilliance when it comes close to sinners. The thrice-holy God is in Jesus the friend of sinners. That's the scandal.

The jealous zeal of God is another aspect of his inner intensity. This jealousy reflects God's passion. God is God, and humanity is only a creature. And this difference is so radical that we tend to misunderstand it. In the power of God, we see strength but fail to see fidelity of heart. In the holiness of God, we see only insurmountable distance, without recognizing that it is, at the same time, tenderness. God is the Almighty and, at the same time, the God of the poor.

In the notion of Father, we fail to see love and begetting, and instead see only power and possessiveness. Evil could be introduced into creation only because God respects humanity and does not impose on us the constraint of holiness. Evil finds its explanation in human freedom. We can always refuse God. But "faith gives us the certainty that God would not permit an evil if he did not cause a good to come from that very evil, by ways that we shall fully know only in eternal life" (*Catechism of the Catholic Church* 324).

God does not ask us to immolate ourselves to make room for his divine power. Rather, God invites us to grow in humility in order to share his power. God descends to humanity to bring humanity into the kingdom of God. Our God is a God to whom humanity can speak an informal "you," as one speaks to a friend. Our God speaks with us. God speaks in prayer. There can be no true prayer unless we are capable of personal initiative in our relationship with God. When we look at Christ, we discover the Father, a Father who loves. The Father loves with his whole being because he is God in his fatherhood. All true love is self-giving, self-emptying. God's love is self-giving in that the Father gives up the Son to the world: "God so loved the world." In his death, Jesus reveals the self-giving of the Father who is one with him. Christ, in his humanity, reveals to us the true face of his Father. It is through such a theology of love that we can correct the false representations of the Father, no longer separating the two Testaments. The entire Old Testament is the story of divine tenderness that chooses a people, delivers it, sanctifies it, and purifies it. The history of Israel strongly manifests the merciful character of God's patient love for his people. We should reread the Book of Hosea. How can our God, who is our Father, not be merciful today to all who are in distress?

To celebrate this merciful tenderness, Scripture speaks of kindness, benevolent fidelity, mercy that forgives. This fatherhood is exercised by God in relation to the Son. Certainly, God the Father did not spare his Son, and yet for the Son, God is first of all mercy and consolation. In the supreme distress of the Son, the Father pours his mercies upon him and raises him up in the infinite consolation of the Holy Spirit. This mercy is linked to the omnipotence of God. Mercy and power are not opposed to one another. Separating them risks betraying the Father's heart. If people of our day are afraid of God, it is because of this opposition that we have introduced. Divine omnipotence is identified with God's fatherhood. It is identified not with a kind of authoritarianism or will to power, but with a gift of infinite life. Here again, the Son reveals the true nature of God's power—it is humble!

There are two conceptions of power: humanity's, which is often close to Satan's, and God's, which is one of service, love, and self-giving. Yes, God's power is manifest in weakness. In Jesus Christ, the omnipotence of God is present in extreme humility, in submission to death. In the Book of Revelation, the all-powerful shepherd becomes a slain lamb that leads the flock:

> For the Lamb at the center of the throne will be their
> shepherd,
> and he will guide them to springs of the water of
> life,
> and God will wipe away every tear from their eyes.
> (Rev 7:17)

A sacrificed shepherd, an immolated lamb, flesh delivered, bread eaten—such is the divine greatness manifest in Jesus.

The parables of mercy—those of the lost sheep, the silver

coin, and the prodigal son—were told by Jesus in the context of his conflict with those who saw themselves as defenders of God's holiness, the scribes and the Pharisees. Those who think they are righteous and reject sinners understand the God of holiness to be very far away. But these people pervert the idea of holiness; they confuse it with the hardness of their own hearts and their own self-righteousness. They forget that God reaches out to sinners to restore the filial relationship. It is through the cross of Jesus that the Father reveals God's divine holiness. Thus holiness brings God closer and manifests itself to us by sanctifying us.

In the same way, God's justice is exerted on us by justifying us. Again, we need to convert our ideas about God's righteousness. The righteousness of God is that of a father. "Righteous Father" (John 17:25; sometimes translated as "Just Father")—this is how the Son speaks to his Father in his priestly prayer. Our Father is not a ruler: "There is no other god besides me, a righteous God and savior" (Isa 45:21). The justice of the Father does not condemn; it is the source of life. It is above all merciful fidelity to God's own saving will. That is why it is the hope of the person in distress.

God does not exercise righteousness or judgment in the human way, distributing punishments and rewards. In the work of salvation, the Father shows righteousness not by demanding a price, but by paying it. The characteristic of God's justice is its self-giving nature. Justice is kind, helpful, and justifying. Certainly, it may seem formidable in its majesty; to consent to it, we must allow ourselves to be formed by the Spirit, even to our depths, which is often difficult.

God chooses not to demand strict justice of humanity, but to save us freely and mercifully. God engages with humanity in the history of salvation. So strict justice is not the last word of God. Beyond strict justice, God is loving and merciful.

Love, which goes beyond justice, does not eliminate justice but includes it. The Father establishes a new order of justice. In

God, justice and mercy are joined. God is just by being faithful to who he is—that is, merciful love. The Father is just with mercy; and with mercy, God does justice to humanity; God gives to humanity what is due to us because God made a covenant with humanity.

The justice of God is indeed an attribute of the love that God *is*. Judgment is only an act of love, for there is no vengeance in God. God responds to evil and sin only through love. God does not "defend himself" either because God has nothing to defend. Because God *is* love, God's love is at once totally vulnerable and totally unassailable—nothing and no one can lessen or take God's love.

> This is the judgment, that the light has come into the world, and people loved darkness rather than light because their deeds were evil. For all who do evil hate the light and do not come to the light, so that their deeds may not be exposed. But those who do what is true come to the light, so that it may be clearly seen that their deeds have been done in God. (John 3:19–21)

This text from John's Gospel is essential. Christ reveals to us that his Father wills only to save. He does not wish to judge; it is humanity who puts itself in a situation of being judged. In reality, humanity judges itself. No person is outside God's love, but a person can say no to love. This is the work of sin. God's judgment consists in this: It is love that respects each person's own judgment of himself and in an act of love ratifies it. There is no judgment for one who believes: "There is no fear in love, but perfect love casts out fear; for fear has to do with punishment, and whoever fears has not reached perfection in love" (1 John 4:18). In John's Gospel, the doctrine of judgment is, in the end, a doctrine of love.

The person who hopes in the Father looks forward to the day of justice impatiently and without fear. "We eagerly wait for the hope of righteousness" (or in some translations, "the hope of justice"), says St. Paul in the Letter to the Galatians (5:5).

This helps us understand the novel insight of St. Thérèse regarding God's justice. In a place and time marked strongly by Jansenism, one of the other sisters in her convent, named Fébronie, defended the rights of divine justice and the idea of offering oneself to God's justice. Thérèse answered her by saying that one can put oneself in relation to God's justice or God's mercy, and by doing so oblige God to act toward her by virtue of his justice or mercy. Only one who stands in relation to merciful love is in relation to the true God, while the other judges herself and forces God to judge her. This is why, as she said, we must arrive in the Father's kingdom empty-handed. "Sister," said Thérèse, "you want God's justice, you will have God's justice. The soul receives exactly what it expects from God."[1]

As for us, let us choose to offer ourselves to God's merciful love and receive precisely that from the Father.

This is the way of freedom! At Notre Dame, because it is the mother church of the archdiocese, we must propose this path. A mother's tenderness helps one discover that of the father. It will take time to purify our erroneous images of God, just as it will take time to show that the church's moral vision is one of happiness, not merely prohibitions and obligations.

The *second priority* is education for freedom. "If you continue in my word, you are truly my disciples; and you will know the truth, and the truth will make you free" (John 8:31–32). It seems to me that education for freedom is the foundation of Christian education.

If many young people find it difficult to engage in professional, family, religious, and civic life, it's because they do not yet have this inner freedom. This is a vast subject that we can't cover adequately here, so I'll just summarize some of what I wrote in another book on educating for freedom.[2]

What are the steps for such an education?

The first step is the discipline of life that we learn in childhood. It is a question of teaching the essential rules that structure a person's life, but also of protecting and nurturing the seed of love that a child carries within himself because he is created in the image and the likeness of God.

First steps are the most important. The work that is done at school is essential. We must value this time of building foundations and, at the same time, never forget what is at stake. It is difficult to build on sand, and failures in early childhood will make future development difficult. This is as true for educating for freedom as it is for intellectual development.

The first causes of youth violence are to be found at this age. Neither indifference nor rigidity effectively form children into free beings, but instead make them either structureless beings or automatons. The teacher has the beautiful mission of helping children discover their talents, maintaining their simplicity and transparency of the heart, conditions that open them to truth. This is to recognize the importance of the interior life.

The child is able at a very young age to descend into her own heart to experience this intimacy with the Lord, to discover a "self deeper than herself" in silence. An awakening of faith happens through this communion with Christ. God the Father, who knows the hearts of his creatures, gave us his Ten Commandments as a first step. This Decalogue does not destroy freedom. In fact, quite the contrary—it begins with love: "You shall love...." Love is our vocation, and both the prohibitions and the obligations of the Ten Commandments are given to protect this gift we have received. Parents are the first educators in this, but teachers too must transmit their experience.

Authority and trust, patience and humor, gentleness and firmness, humility and kindness—all are qualities that belong to an effective educator.

The second step is adolescence. This is a difficult but exciting stage of progress. It is important here to begin to understand better and follow more closely the path of virtue, which is described well in the heritage of "the humanities," but which is further enlightened by the word of God and nourished by the sacraments. Especially important here are cardinal and theological virtues, and the gifts and the fruits of the Holy Spirit.

The qualities of an effective educator, for this step, are accompaniment and a closeness that is tempered with appropriate distance and self-control. The 2018 Synod on Young People, Faith, and Vocational Discernment emphasized the importance of accompaniment for discernment, not only regarding religious vocations but for engagement in the whole of life. Young people seek effective, trustworthy, faith-filled guides, imitators of Christ living truly happy lives that nourish a relationship with God and with the church. Our teens cannot do it alone. Such accompaniment is marked by listening and dialogue.

Listening implies availability. There is "a time for everything" in education, and it takes time! Sometimes educators want to see immediate progress. But often, to paraphrase Psalm 126, one teacher will sow in tears while another, later, will reap with shouts of joy. Though it's true that it's wonderful to be the one to reap from time to time.

But the process is not just about listening; it's about educating. We cannot be silent. Our young people need reliable guidance. There is advice to give, as well as instruction. Starting from their own experience, to help understand what did and did not work well, is useful. I like St. Teresa of Avila's comment, "Holiness is falling down and getting back up."

Obviously, she doesn't mean that we should seek to fall, but that we should get up again when we do. The process of education is beautiful, even if it is sometimes exhausting. We must help young people develop the virtue of prudence. Too many of our teens, manipulated by what they hear and see, can no longer discern what is true. We must give them the means for such discernment. This means being close to them, while respecting their space as well. I am pleased to see that educators are providing leisure time, too. Youth organizations are reappearing in the parishes—it's marvelous!

This accompaniment of young people will help the hope of Don Bosco to be realized: "That young people not only are loved, but that they *know* they are loved." But for that to happen, fathers must be fathers, mothers must be mothers, teachers must be teachers, and priests must be fathers, too! We can't pretend to be big brothers! Because if it seems at first that we've been welcomed as part of the "teen tribe," we will soon be rejected; they expect something different from us—even if they sometimes turn a deaf ear!

Self-control is, in fact, an important quality. Adolescence is a tumultuous period in which the young person oscillates between being a child and being an adult, being pleasant and unpleasant, being logical and irrational—and often all in the same day. He will seek to get a rise out of a teacher or other adult, to exploit weakness, to push boundaries. Responding with anger is rarely worthwhile; one can try to tamp down a teen's anger, but it will only be repressed in his heart. We must teach young people to express their anger maturely and constructively.

To guide a young person to discover his freedom, a teacher must avoid any sort of possessiveness. A teacher doesn't own her students, just as parents don't own their children. They are gifts. The educator who forgets that ends up suppressing the freedom of the young people entrusted to him.

If the Ten Commandments correspond to the period of foundation-building, the Sermon on the Mount (presented in Matt 5—7) corresponds to the period of formation, of progress. In this text, Jesus criticizes the legalistic morality of the Pharisees, preoccupied with the negative precepts of the Decalogue. By analogy, education must go beyond prohibitions and obligations. It must advance the qualities of the heart and thus lead to the truth. Sometimes, when young people fail to advance beyond the first stage, adolescence becomes a crisis with difficult consequences. The Sermon on the Mount is surely more difficult to live than the Decalogue, but Christ gives grace to live it.

The third and final stage is maturity. It generally should correspond to the final year of high school. Unfortunately, entry into adulthood is more and more delayed in our day, precisely because of this lack of freedom. Let us keep in mind these three signs of interior freedom:

- to develop and integrate a self-awareness and awareness of others;
- to develop and integrate a healthy interiority and externality;
- to develop and integrate a way of living "for oneself" and "for others."

These three criteria summarize Christian education. This is the heart of evangelization.

It is true that educating young people is not one of the specific aspects of the mission of the Cathedral. This occurs naturally in the family, as well as in schools, parishes, and elsewhere. But many parents come to tell us of their difficulties and sometimes their suffering, and we are here not only to offer them to the Lord but to offer them the guidance they seek. Many young people come to ask us questions about their future. It seems to me that the Cathedral must be an educator and participate in the training of people who can effectively accompany them. Pope Francis insists on such ministry.

16

A PRIEST FIRST

I STARTED THIS BOOK by telling you about what I *do*. But perhaps I should have started by telling you who I *am*. These last pages are a testimony of what is most important in my life. My ministry over the years has included the formation of priests, their spiritual accompaniment, and their ongoing formation. The friendship of priests is very important to me. We receive many priests here at Notre Dame—this includes priests of the Archdiocese of Paris, simply because this is their Cathedral, their home; priests from elsewhere in France or other nations because they come to enjoy the spiritual or liturgical setting; other priests who come with their choirs or pilgrimage groups; and finally, priests who come to receive the sacrament of reconciliation. Indeed, priests frequently come to the Cathedral for confession—starting with the rector!

In this last chapter, I wish to share with you some convictions that give me life. I don't intend to offer a portrait of what the perfect priest is like. Is there such a thing anyway? The Curé of Ars perhaps, but even he had his limitations and weaknesses.

Since my ordination in June 1980, three beautiful popes have nourished my theology of the priesthood: John Paul II, the pope of hope; Benedict XVI, the pope of faith; and Francis, the pope of love. All three of these shepherds have provided guidance that shapes my ministry, especially at Notre Dame.

"Certainly there is an essential aspect of the priest that does not change: the priest of tomorrow, no less than the priest of today, must resemble Christ," said St. John Paul II.[1] That's why he liked to say to priests, "We want to see Jesus through you."

The wonder of the beginning, the vocation, gift and mystery. John Paul II tells us the story of his own vocation, his spiritual path, the accompaniment of his spiritual father. Yes, what a mystery! Why us? No doubt we will have the answer when we arrive in the kingdom.

"We have been called! This is the fundamental truth that must instill courage and joy in us!" he told a group of priests on one occasion.[2]

Each priest is called in the most personal way. Every priest has his own story. I heard the call on the day of my first communion, at seven years old. I often say that I have been nourished with the water of Lourdes, so much that the Blessed Virgin is part of this call. But it is Christ who calls and who gives the means to accomplish the mission he entrusts to us. Throughout our priestly life, there are successive calls. The priest exercises his ministry in a spirit of renunciation like the useless servant, desiring nothing more than to do the Master's will.

We have been chosen to be with Christ, and we need to deepen this relationship of friendship with the Lord. John Paul II was a model. Those who had the grace to pray with him in his private chapel saw a pope who carried the world on his shoulders—a truly sacerdotal intercessory prayer. Prayer was the heart of his life.

This was undoubtedly the secret of his transfigured face, of that smile that expressed his inner peace and joy. The question of priestly vocations was for him a real preoccupation. A holy priest is calling! In his first letter to the priests, on Holy Thursday 1979, St. John Paul evoked the image of a parish without priests:

> Think of the places where people anxiously await a Priest, and where for many years; feeling the lack of such a Priest, they do not cease to hope for his presence. And sometimes it happens that they meet in an abandoned shrine, and place on the altar a stole which they still keep, and recite all the prayers of the Eucharistic liturgy; and then, at the moment that corresponds to the transubstantiation a deep silence comes down upon them, a silence sometimes broken by a sob...so ardently do they desire to hear the words that only the lips of a Priest can efficaciously utter.[3]

I often meditate on this text, thinking of so many French parishes that no longer have a priest. What a sorrow!

Priestly ordination does not confer merely a mission in the church, but a new consecration—we become another Christ. We must rekindle this gift. As John Paul II said, "The priest participates ontologically in the priesthood of Christ, the man of holiness....He shares with his brothers and sisters what is sacred: truth, the grace of God. This is the true priestly identity. This is the essential requirement of priestly ministry."[4]

This gift of the priesthood is not given for the priest, but for the church, for the people entrusted to him. The bishop sends priests where they are needed. Certainly, there can be dialogue about this between the bishop and the priest, if only to confirm the priest's aptitude to take on the mission the bishop has in mind. But accepting the bishop's will is one way for the priest to enter into the obedience of Christ and to remember that he does not choose his own mission.

Obviously, then, the priest is called to holiness. "Each one of you must be holy, and help his brothers fulfill their vocation to holiness."[5] Our first means of sanctification is the ministry itself, in which priestly grace is expressed. The priest is transformed by the word he proclaims. He is sanctified by the celebration of the sacraments, which strengthens him in faith and in his union with Christ. Finally, by exercising pastoral charity, he unifies his heart.

"The priest must have a soul radiant with beauty whose light enlightens and rejoices the souls of those who have their eyes turned toward him," said the fourth-century bishop and doctor of the church St. John Chrysostom in his treatise on the priesthood. That is why the priest must have a spiritual director who will encourage him and help him to be truthful about himself. And what a grace this is for the spiritual director! Accompanying many priests at the request of my bishop, I can confide that these are moments of grace.

The path of holiness is that of humility and obedience. Pride leads to clericalism; humility reminds all, priests and laity alike, that we are only servants. Obedience is a fruit of priestly grace; it allows us to understand that the mission does not belong to us. It is a way of living chastity as a gift. Celibacy is a challenge to the mentality of our time. Some would like to see the marriage of priests as the miracle solution to the vocations crisis. But this is a dream. What I'm sure of is that if I were married, my dear wife and children would not see me very much. Celibacy must be lived as a gift. Linked to celibacy, the spirit of poverty guarantees our spiritual freedom.

John Paul II, during a retreat to priests, said, "Only the priest who possesses Christ, because he desires him, loves him, is in intimate and permanent and progressive communion of life with him, becomes a 'witness' and therefore a credible 'evangelizer.'"[6]

We are priests above all for the Eucharist. St. John Paul II commented that a priest is as effective as his life is eucharistic, and he added, "Mass without love, a sterile priest; fervent Mass, a priest who conquers souls; Eucharistic devotion neglected and without love, a priest in danger of being lost."[7]

What a grace it is for we who are priests to be able to celebrate the Eucharist every day. It is our strength. It focuses us on what is most essential. It is the heart of our priestly life. The Eucharist is the ideal of the life of the priest. He must become, like Christ, both a priest and victim, to quote St. Thomas Aquinas. Eucharistic adoration also helps the priest to configure himself to Christ, so that he is able to become all things to all people.

The priest is also a witness of God's tenderness as a servant of mercy. St. John Paul II reiterated this, saying, "To evoke conversion and penance in man's heart and to offer him the gift of reconciliation is the specific mission of the church as she continues the redemptive work of her divine founder."[8]

As you can see, this holy pope centered his theology of priesthood on the holy character received at ordination. The priest is not merely a functionary; he is first configured to Christ, the one high priest. This is his point of departure for developing the spiritual and sacramental life. We understand, then, his concern to bring the priests back to the source, so that they rediscover their identity. Older priests sometimes have trouble understanding the next generation of priests; but they are precisely those formed during the pontificate of John Paul II, which explains why they feel compelled to show and express their joy at being priests.

We are sent to seek the lost sheep, to lead them to the living springs of salvation. The priest is called to feed the flock by preaching the gospel and by teaching. This is why he must walk at the speed of the flock, being attentive to the sheep that are out of breath and that step off the path. This is true pastoral charity. This calls for real availability, an understanding of humanity, the patience of a shepherd, attentiveness to wounded hearts with a look of hope. A priest is able to adopt such a look only as the fruit of contemplative prayer that allows him to see people as God sees them.

And John Paul II tells us that in thinking of the priesthood, we cannot forget the place of Mary, the mother of priests: "In the midst of the People of God, that looks to Mary with immense love and hope, you must look to her with exceptional hope and love....You must nourish human hearts with Christ: and who can make you more aware of what you are doing than she who nourished him?"[9] Mary is the mother of priests, and like all mothers, she watches over the spiritual life of the priests of her Son. Because he is minister of the sacrament of mercy, Mary—who, by her tenderness and intercession with sinners, leads us to the source of merciful love—is close to the priest. It is not a coincidence that Christ on the cross entrusted his Mother to the priest John. As John Paul II said, "John responded immediately to the invitation of Christ and took Mary with him....He showed himself to be a 'true priest,' yes, a faithful follower of Jesus."[10]

As priests, we need his presence: "For every priest, to take Mary into his home means to make a place for her in his life by remaining in a habitual union with her through his thoughts, his affections, his zeal for the Kingdom of God, and his worship."[11]

The fruitfulness of our priestly ministry is at stake. Mary helps us to constantly repeat her *fiat*, to live the evangelical virtues, to renew our consecration. John Paul II shares his priestly experience: "In our 'ministerial' priesthood there is the wonderful and penetrating dimension of nearness to the Mother of Christ. So let us try to live in that dimension. If I may be permitted to speak here of my own experience, I will say to you that in writing to you I am referring especially to my own personal experience."[12]

"*Totus Tuus*" ("Totally Yours")—the motto of St. John Paul II—is imbued with the conviction that the surest way to belong totally to Christ is to devote oneself body and soul to the Virgin Mary.

Let's leave St. John Paul II and turn to Pope Benedict XVI, whose pontificate included a special year dedicated to the priesthood (2010). Benedict continued the teaching of his predecessor, starting from the priest's very being. Recalling the expression of the Curé of Ars, "the priesthood is the love of the heart of Jesus," Benedict presented the priesthood as a gift: "This touching expression makes us reflect, first of all, with heartfelt gratitude on the immense gift which priests represent, not only for the Church, but also for humanity itself."[13] No, the pope does not want to make priests proud, but to make us more aware of the greatness of the priesthood and therefore of our responsibility.

The consecration of the priest is a gift of grace received on the day of his ordination. The more he becomes aware of this gift, the more he will live, the more he will produce fruit. To constantly rekindle his consecration, the priest must let himself be molded by the Word of truth. "Consecrate them in the truth" (John 17:17, NABRE), says Jesus to his Father in his priestly prayer.

This consecration is a true transformation of the priest's being. St. Gregory of Nyssa says that the priest is changed "for the better." But we also know that grace does not destroy nature. That is why, throughout his priestly life, the priest must continue to let himself be seized by Christ, so that he may come to say with St. Paul, "It is no longer I who live, but it is Christ who lives in me" (Gal 2:20). It is clear that, for Pope Benedict, the absolute primacy of divine grace is the foundation of his theology of the priesthood. (What a joy it is for me to be able to exercise my ministry in the very place where I was ordained!)

Before even speaking of the mission of the priest, of his ministry, of what he must do, Benedict XVI returns to his being: "The missionary dimension of the priesthood is born from the priest's sacramental configuration to Christ....Through the imposition of the Bishop's hands and the consecratory prayer of the Church, the candidates become new men, they become 'presbyters.'"[14] This is what we find in the gospel—Christ calls his disciples *first* to be with him, and *then* to proclaim the word. One must first experience the closeness to Christ, to identify with him. We have to continue his mission, but it is necessary to live with Christ to understand it well.

We must therefore give our attention not so much to what the priest *does* but to what the priest *is*. Moreover, this is the element that will catch the interest of young people—moreso, anyway, than seeing a priest's constant busyness and unrestrained activism at the risk of forgetting what is most essential, his friendship with Christ.

Recounting his own vocation and his ordination, Pope Benedict said,

> On the eve of my priestly ordination, fifty-eight years ago, I opened the Sacred Scripture, because I wanted to receive once more a word from the Lord for that day and for my future journey as a priest. My gaze fell on this passage: "Sanctify them in the truth; your word is truth." Then I realized: the Lord is speaking about me, and he is speaking to me. This very same thing will be accomplished tomorrow in me. When all is said and done, we are not consecrated by rites, even though rites are necessary. The bath in which the Lord immerses us is himself—the Truth in person.[15]

The ritual of the imposition of hands, so beautiful, so mysterious, accompanied by the beautiful prayer pronounced by the bishop, is often underlined by sacred silence. At Notre Dame, it is accompanied by the ringing of bells that announce to the people of Paris the gift of grace that is being received at the Cathedral. And there is the rite of the anointing of the hands, "so that they could become hands of blessing," as Benedict said. "Let us pray to the Lord at this hour that our hands will serve more and more to bring salvation, to bring blessing, to make his goodness present!"[16]

This consecration identifies the priest with Christ. Thus, it is not the priest who evangelizes, but Christ, and the priest must participate in the life of Christ, living and celebrating his sacrifice in the Eucharist, in order for his proclamation to be authentic.

The liturgy, then, is the source of the priest's identity and life. It is there that he clothes himself in Christ and that he speaks and acts "*in persona Christi*," that is, Christ is the subject, the celebrant, of the liturgy he celebrates. Pope Benedict wrote, "Priests should be conscious of the fact that in their ministry they must never put themselves or their personal opinions in first place, but Jesus Christ."[17] This means that the liturgy does not belong to us; we cannot do with it as we wish. The priest who presides must know how to step aside so that Christ is seen at the heart of the liturgy.

We know how important the liturgy is for Benedict XVI. One of my greatest joys as a priest was to be part of the team preparing the Mass celebrated by him at Les Invalides and then the celebration of Vespers at Notre Dame, during his apostolic journey to Paris. During a preparatory meeting at the Vatican with his master of ceremonies, I asked what would please the Holy Father. The answer was clear: during the recessional for Vespers at Notre Dame, play a work by the French composer Olivier Messiaen, and during the Mass at Les Invalides, make sure there are two periods of silence—one after the homily and the other after the communion. Silence in the presence of the 260,000 people expected at Les Invalides seemed unlikely!

Before leaving the sacristy as Mass was beginning at Les Invalides, at the moment of the departure of the procession, the pope repeated to me his desire: "Don't forget to ask for silence after the homily and after communion." I did this after the homily, but it turned out not even to be necessary after communion; the prayerful presence of Benedict, his own recollection, was a call to attentive silence. He himself was deeply touched by the silence of that assembly.

Pope Benedict was often critical of those who disfigured the eucharistic celebration, transforming it into a spectacle.

"The life of the liturgy does not consist in 'pleasant' surprises and attractive 'ideas' but in solemn repetitions," he said prior to becoming pope.[18] It is through these solemn repetitions that the holiness of God manifests itself. It is necessary in the liturgy to receive what is given and not to manufacture a product. He said, "In the liturgy there is a power, an energy at work which not even the Church as a whole can generate: what it manifests is the Wholly Other, coming to us through the community."[19] I witness this every day at the Cathedral—even at the less solemn weekday Masses, the Wholly Other is made present and sweeps us up.

As he said to the priests of the Diocese of Albano, "It seems to me that people truly feel that we converse with God, with them, and that in this common prayer we attract others, in communion with the children of God we attract others; or if not, we are only doing something superficial."[20]

All our lives are prayer, with the Mass as their center, but we must also take the time to dwell with Christ. "The priest who prays a lot, and who prays well," said Pope Benedict, "is progressively drawn out of himself and evermore united to Jesus the Good Shepherd and the Servant of the Brethren."[21] St. Charles Borromeo said, "You will not be able to heal the souls of others if you let your own wither. You must have time for yourself to be with God." The priest must remember this all the time, especially if he is very busy! It is these times of prayer that will allow him to be close to wounded humanity. "The priest," Benedict said, "enter[s], like Christ, into human wretchedness, carr[ies] it with him, visit[s] those who are suffering and look[s] after them."[22]

A priest's compassion is rooted in the mercy he has experienced in his own life, before ministering to others. What a beautiful call to holiness! Addressing seminarians, Benedict told them that their time of formation needed to be "years of interior silence, of unceasing prayer, of constant study." He continued,

"We have to be saints so as not to create a contradiction between the sign that we are and the reality that we wish to signify."[23]

When Benedict XVI announced that he was retiring into a life of silence, it was a real thunderclap. Some thought the decision was courageous; others thought he was running away. It was an act of the same kind of humility and poverty that he had preached about to priests himself. The decision was for the good of the church. Even today, Benedict, in his monastery residence in the Vatican Gardens, is not inactive. He has a beautiful mission, that of carrying the church in his prayer.

All that he told us about the priesthood reflected what he himself learned in prayerful silence. On the day of his first Mass as Peter's successor, he said, "At this moment there is no need for me to present a program of governance....My real program of governance is not to do my own will, not to pursue my own ideas, but to listen, together with the whole Church, to the word and the will of the Lord, to be guided by Him."[24]

In announcing his retirement, he told the cardinals that it was the fruit of his prayer, that it was the will of God that he had discerned. What a great example for the rector, who will leave his responsibilities when he turns seventy-five, not because he chooses to, but because it is the mandatory retirement age.

Since the election of Pope Francis, we have been a bit jostled, even surprised, because he comes from another continent and seems to have a hard time understanding our old Europe.

Reform the Vatican dicasteries, yes, but the fundamental reform is the reform of hearts, and that takes time. It is true that our pope does not mince words and, according to the Ignatian method, that he often asks us questions, inviting us to an examination of conscience. At first glance, we might be tempted to say that he does not encourage us priests much and that he makes us feel guilty. But if you look closely, it becomes clear that he does it out of love. More than his predecessors, Pope Francis works at the pastoral level, with images that are affectionate and that touch hearts. Of course, all pastoral ministry rests on theology, and Francis's theology of the priesthood is not revolutionary; it is part of a continuity, though with different accents.

I was touched by the homily he preached at the Chrism Mass of Holy Week 2014, when he said to his brother priests,

> The Lord anointed us in Christ with the oil of gladness....*A joy which anoints us.* In a word: it has penetrated deep within our hearts, it has shaped them and strengthened them sacramentally....Grace fills us to the brim and overflows, fully, abundantly and entirely in each priest. We are anointed down to our very bones...and our joy, which wells up from deep within, is the echo of this anointing.[25]

Here we find an echo of the teaching of St. John Paul II and Benedict XVI. The priest is configured to Christ the Priest, and he must radiate the joy that dwells in him. The pope returns to this idea often. Why do Christians have "funeral faces" when they go to Mass? Why do some look like "pickled peppers"? The priest is a servant of joy, and he must allow that joy to shine!

Pope Francis speaks of that "imperishable joy" that "can lie dormant, or be clogged by sin or by life's troubles, yet deep down it remains intact, like the embers of a burnt log beneath the ashes, and it can always be renewed."[26]

Finally, it is a missionary joy: "Priestly joy is deeply bound up with God's holy and faithful people, for it is an eminently missionary joy."[27]

Pope Francis acts as a pastor, and through all his public comments on priesthood, it is always to place the priest in relation to his people. There is a shared life between him and his parishioners. He knows the smell of his sheep. The pope continues on the theme of joy: "The priest is poor in terms of purely human joy. He has given up so much! And because he is poor, he, who gives so much to others, has to seek his joy from the Lord and from God's faithful people."[28]

The priest's joy is his gift because there is always more joy in giving than in receiving, but it is also a joy in the people that his bishop has entrusted to him. If the priest is not happy, it is because he does not perceive that he is loved and welcomed. The greatest joy of the pastor comes on Sunday when he meets his people. It is a spiritual apex; he is there to welcome, to listen, to receive news that will become part of his priestly prayer.

Francis continues on the topic of joy: "*Priestly joy is a joy which is sister to fidelity*. Not primarily in the sense that we are all 'immaculate' (would that by God's grace we were!), for we are sinners, but in the sense of an ever renewed fidelity to the one Bride, to the Church. Here fruitfulness is key."[29] When I was director of the seminary, I always said to those preparing for priesthood, "When you are prostrate on the floor and then hands are imposed on you, ask for the grace of fidelity. It is this fidelity that is a source of joy, and that joy will shine on your faces."

Finally, Francis says, "*Priestly joy is a joy which is sister to obedience*. An obedience to the Church in the hierarchy which gives us, as it were, not simply the external framework for our obedience: the parish to which I am sent, my ministerial assignments, my particular work...but also union with God the Father, the source of all fatherhood."[30]

So the pope encourages us to live the evangelical counsels not as a burden, but as a joy that must be reflected! This is the very concrete advice he gives us for exercising our ministry, and as always, it is very didactic and colorful.

The pope exhorted seminarians preparing for priesthood in Rome: "To go forth, go forth! For me this is the kernel of evangelization. And going forth means going somewhere, that is, closeness." This theme of pastoral closeness is dear to him. "If you don't go out of yourself you will never reach closeness! Closeness. To be close to people, to be close to everyone, to all those to whom we should be close. All people. Go forth. Closeness. One cannot evangelize without closeness!"[31]

You may have seen the photograph of Cardinal Bergoglio on the subway in Buenos Aires, talking to the man sitting next to him. To evangelize, one must actually listen to people's hopes, needs, and aspirations. If we remain in the sacristy, we will not be able to encounter people who no longer ask anything of the church. And the pope develops this proximity: "Closeness with kindness; the closeness of love, also physical closeness."[32]

This proximity is reflected in a priest's preaching. The pope has very clear ideas on the homily; they must be short, with an image that catches the attention of those present:

> The problem with boring homilies—so to speak—the problem with boring homilies is that there is no closeness. It is precisely in the homily that we measure a pastor's closeness to his people. If in the homily you speak, let's say, 20, 25 or 30, 40 minutes—these aren't fantasies, this happens!—and you speak of abstract things, of truths of the faith, you are not delivering a homily, you are playing school! That is different! You are not close to the people. That is why the homily is important: calibrate it, get an idea of how close the priest is.[33]

It must be said that the literary genre of homilies is not easy to teach. Some priests have gifts for this. Others have more difficulty; in this case, let it be short and let your heart speak while preparing the homily.

Addressing priests involved in the charismatic renewal movement, the pope returned to this theme:

> To you priests I would say just one word: closeness. Closeness to Jesus Christ, in prayer and adoration. Closeness to the Lord, and closeness to people, to God's people who have been entrusted to you. Love your people, stay close to them. This is what I ask of you, this double closeness: to Jesus and to people.[34]

For the pope, there is always a balance between pastoral care and spirituality. He said this to the members of the Congregation for the Clergy:

> This is what it means to "be" priests, it is not just limited to what priests "do"; they are free from all spiritual worldliness, conscious that their life is first and foremost about evangelizing even before their work.
>
> How beautiful it is to see priests joyous in their vocation, with a deep serenity, that sustains them even in moments of fatigue and pain! And this never comes about without prayer, prayer from the heart, from that dialogue with the Lord...who is the heart, so to speak, of priestly life. We need priests, there is a lack of vocations.[35]

And the pope sets an example—every evening, before dinner, he spends an hour in prayer before the Blessed Sacrament. He says his prayer time is "always full of memory, of recollection."[36] The pope then returns to the moral life of the priests and offers an examination of conscience. Again, it is not to make us feel guilty, but ultimately to protect us from the devil, whom the pope never hesitates to warn us about.

He says,

> This is a good examination of conscience for a priest: if the Lord were to return today, where would he find me? "For where your treasure is, there will your heart be also" (Mt 6:21). And where is my heart? Is it among the people, praying with and for the people, involved with their joys and sufferings, or is it rather among worldly things, earthly affairs, in my private "spaces"? A priest cannot have a private space, because he is always either with the Lord or with the people. I think of those priests that I knew in my city, when there were no answering machines, who slept with a phone on the bedside table. At whatever time people would call, they got up to give the anointing: no one died without the sacraments![37]

During one of his weekday Masses at the St. Martha Residence, he offered as an example a priest who knew all his parishioners by name, even the names of their dogs. This too is evangelization.

But he warns us of obstacles and temptations along our path. Is he reproaching us when he does this? No, he is calling us to holiness. The first pitfall he warns us about is careerism. The second is pride. Echoing St. Titus, Francis warns

> that the priest—whether a priest or bishop—be blameless; not be arrogant, not look down on everyone; not

> be quick-tempered, but be meek, not a drunkard, spiritual not irreverent; that he not be violent but peaceful; not greedy for gain, not attached to money, but hospitable, a lover of goodness, upright, just, holy, self-controlled, holding firm to the sure word as taught.[38]

While the pope helps us examine our consciences, he also wants to be encouraging because he loves priests. He says we only remember "a small handful of the many holy bishops, the many priests, the many holy priests" who have dedicated "their entire lives to the service of the diocese, of the parish." There have been so many "anonymous parish priests whom we do not know....Parish priests in the countryside and parish priests in the city who by their anointing gave their people strength, transmitted doctrine, conferred the sacraments; that is, holiness."[39] And in his own direct style, Francis commented,

> "But, Father, I read in the newspaper that a bishop did such, or that a priest did such and such!" "Yes, I read it too! But tell me: do the newspapers print all the good that so many priests do, so many priests in so many parishes in the city and countryside? The charity they show? The work they do to carry their people forward?" No, this isn't news! The proverb still holds true: "A single tree falling in the forest causes more sound than an entire forest that slowly grows and matures."[40]

In another homily at the St. Martha Residence, he said, "It is beautiful to find priests who have given their lives as priests. Priests of whom the people say: 'But yes, he has a bit of a temper, he's got this and that, but he is a priest!' And the people have a nose about these things!"[41]

Addressing the Italian bishops' conference, Francis painted a marvelous picture of the pastor:

> He is not scandalized by the frailties that shake the human soul: aware that he is himself a healed paralytic, he is far removed from the coldness of the rigorist....Having given up self-determination, he has no agenda to protect, but each morning consigns his time to the Lord so as to be free to meet and be approached by people....A servant of life, he walks with the heart and pace of the poor; he is enriched by being with them. He is a man of peace and reconciliation, a sign and instrument of God's tenderness, careful to spread goodness with the same fervor with which others look after their own interests.[42]

The priest shares this tenderness most of all through the sacrament of penance. By promulgating the Jubilee Year of Mercy, the pope was able to address priests again:

> Never tire of being merciful! Please! Have the ability to forgive that the Lord had, who came not to condemn but to forgive! Be greatly merciful! And if you have scruples about being too "forgiving," think of that holy priest about whom I have told you, who went before the Tabernacle and said: "Lord, pardon me if I have forgiven too much, but it is you who have set me a bad example!"[43]

After a long period of hearing confessions, I like to repeat this sentence, which sounds a lot like Don Camillo!

That is why the pope insists that the confessional must not be a place of torture. He said once to an audience of priests, "I ask you...to be pastors with the compassion of God. To leave the 'whip' hanging in the sacristy and to be pastors with tenderness, [even] with those who create many problems."[44]

To the missionaries of mercy, in February 2016, the pope gave advice regarding the sacrament:

> Several months ago I was speaking with a wise Cardinal of the Roman Curia about the questions that some priests ask when hearing confession, and he told me: "When people start and I see that they want to unburden themselves, and I realize that I understand it, I tell them, 'I understand! Stay calm!'" So go ahead. This is a father.[45]

I will conclude with a last bit of advice from Pope Francis, offered to a group of seminarians, on priestly friendship:

> Seek this, it is important. Be friends. I think this helps a great deal in living the priestly life, the spiritual life, the apostolic life, community life and also the intellectual life: priestly friendship. If I were to meet a priest who said to me: "I have never had a friend," I would think that this priest has not had one of the most beautiful joys of the priestly life: priestly friendship.

And then the pope concluded,

> This is my hope for you. I hope that you be friends with those whom the Lord places along your path as friends. I wish you this in life. Priestly friendship is a force for perseverance, apostolic joy, courage, and even for humor. It is beautiful, most beautiful! This is what I think.[46]

Our Cathedral is, I hope, a place of priestly friendship.

And if, by chance, a young man who is considering the question of the priesthood reads these few pages, what I would say to him is that a priest sacrifices everything—except happiness. You can understand—I think, I hope—through all these quotations the priestly ideal that all priests try to reach. Each of us knows that there is always a way to go to reach it. And the people who work with me know it well!

NOTES

CHAPTER 1

1. Pope Francis, "Address to Rectors and Students of the Pontifical Colleges and Residences of Rome" (May 12, 2014), http://w2.vatican.va/content/francesco/en/speeches/2014/may/documents/papa-francesco_20140512_pontifici-collegi-convitti.html.

2. *Catechism of the Catholic Church* (New York: Doubleday, 1994, 1997).

3. Address to the bishops of Chile (July 13, 1988).

CHAPTER 2

1. [The author uses a play on words in the original French here: "*l'écran fait écran*," literally: "the screen is a screen." –Trans.]

2. Georges Bernanos, *The Diary of a Country Priest*, trans. Pamela Morris (London: Boriswood, 1937), 151–52.

3. *Story of a Soul: The Autobiography of St. Thérèse of Lisieux*, trans. John Clarke, OCD (Washington, DC: ICS Publications, 1975), 180.

4. LT 266, to Fr. Bellière, Archives du Carmel de Lisieux (August 25, 1897), http://www.archives-carmel-lisieux.fr/english/carmel/index.php/lt-261-a-266/1178-lt-266-a-labbe-belliere.

5. Robert J. Edmonson, ed. and trans., *The Complete Thérèse of Lisieux* (Brewster, MA: Paraclete Press, 2009), 291–92.

CHAPTER 3

1. Pope Benedict XVI, "Homily at Vespers with Priests, Religious, Seminarians, and Deacons" (September 12, 2008), http://www.vatican.va/content/benedict-xvi/en/homilies/2008/documents/hf_ben-xvi_hom_20080912_parigi-vespri.html.

CHAPTER 4

1. Paul Claudel, "December 25, 1886," trans. Wallace Fowlie, *Poetry* 87, no. 3 (December 1955): 143–46. All the following quoted passages from this poem are from this translation. The French original can be found in Paul Claudel, *Oeuvre poétique* (Paris: Gallimard, 1957) and also Claudel, *Poésies* (Paris: Gallimard, 1970).

2. Paul Claudel, "Third Ode: Magnificat," in *Five Great Odes*, trans. Edward Lucie-Smith (Chester Springs, PA: Dufour Editions, 1967), 50–51.

3. Paul Claudel, "The Virgin at Noon," trans. Wallace Fowlie, *Poetry* 87, no. 3 (December 1955): 138–39.

CHAPTER 5

1. Pope John Paul II, "Address to UNESCO," *L'Osservatore Romano*, English weekly edition, June 23, 1980, 9–12, http://inters.org/John-Paul-II-UNESCO-Culture.

2. Georges Bernanos, *Tradition of Freedom* (London: Dennis Dobson, 1950), 117, 118, 132.

3. Paul Claudel, *Positions et Propositions*, vol. 1 (Paris: Gallimard, 1934), 166.

4. Ernest Renan, *L'avenir de la science: pensées de 1848* (Paris: Calmann-Lévy, 1890), 238.

5. André Vingt-Trois et al., *Notre-Dame de Paris*, La grâce d'une cathédrale series (Paris: Editions Place des Victoires, 2012), 289.

CHAPTER 7

1. [An important Catholic study center in Paris that offers rich theological and biblical courses, conferences, and dialogues. It was founded as a Carmelite monastery and college in the mid-thirteenth century. –Trans.]

2. [The reason for the confusion is clear in French but not in English: *Parabole* is the French word for the English *parable*, but it is also an informal word for the English *satellite dish*. –Trans.]

3. [The English word *thirtieth* is *trentième* in French, which is close to *Trente*, the French version of the name of the city of Trent (site of the sixteenth-century ecumenical council). –Trans.]

CHAPTER 8

1. [There is a well-known statue of Isabelle Romée, Joan of Arc's mother, located in Domrémy, her hometown, about 200 miles from Paris. –Trans.]

CHAPTER 9

1. [Pepita was a girl who Victor Hugo knew as a child in Spain. Adele was Hugo's wife. –Trans.]

2. Victor Hugo, *The Hunchback of Notre-Dame* (Philadelphia: Running Press, 1995), 238.

3. [A line from Victor Hugo's poetry collection, *Les Contemplations*. –Trans.]

4. Hugo, *The Hunchback of Notre-Dame*, 567.

5. Hugo, *The Hunchback of Notre-Dame*, 567.

6. Hugo, *The Hunchback of Notre-Dame*, 568–69.

7. Hugo, *The Hunchback of Notre-Dame*, 569.

CHAPTER 10

1. [All of this was written by the author prior to the disastrous fire at Notre Dame on April 15, 2019. –Trans.]

2. [A famous hospital that stands next to Notre Dame Cathedral. Founded in the seventh century by St. Landry, it is the oldest hospital in the city of Paris and remains a symbol of charity and hospitality. –Trans.]

3. [The two main characters in a well-known 1950s French-Italian film, *Le Petit Monde de don Camillo* (The Little World of Fr. Camillo), who were constantly quarrelling with each other. –Trans.]

CHAPTER 13

1. Pope Paul VI, apostolic exhortation *Evangelii Nuntiandi* (December 8, 1975), http://www.vatican.va/content/paul-vi/en/apost_exhortations/documents/hf_p-vi_exh_19751208_evangelii-nuntiandi.html.

2. Pope Francis, Angelus address (July 15, 2018, corrected), http://www.vatican.va/content/francesco/en/angelus/2018/documents/papa-francesco_angelus_20180715.html.

CHAPTER 14

1. Georges Bernanos, *Tradition of Freedom* (London: Dennis Dobson, 1950), 118.

2. Bernanos, *Tradition of Freedom*, 145, 149.

3. Pope John Paul II, encyclical letter *Redemptoris Missio* (December 7, 1990), no. 90, http://www.vatican.va/content/john-paul-ii/en/encyclicals/documents/hf_jp-ii_enc_07121990_redemptoris-missio.html.

CHAPTER 15

1. *Letters of St. Thérèse of Lisieux: Volume II, 1890–1897*, trans. John Clarke (Washington, DC: Institute of Carmelite Studies, 1988), 737.

2. Patrick Chauvet, *Eduquer des êtres libres* (Les Plans-sur-Bex: Parole et silence, 2001).

CHAPTER 16

1. Pope John Paul II, post-synodal apostolic exhortation *Pastores Dabo Vobis* (March 25, 1992), no. 5, http://www.vatican.va/content/john-paul-ii/en/apost_exhortations/documents/hf_jp-ii_exh_25031992_pastores-dabo-vobis.html.

2. Pope John Paul II, Address to a Group of Priests from the Archdiocese of Milan (April 21, 1979), http://www.vatican.va/content/john-paul-ii/en/speeches/1979/april/documents/hf_jp-ii_spe_19790421_sacerdoti-milano.html.

3. Pope John Paul II, *Letter to Priests on the Occasion of Holy Thursday 1979* (April 9, 1979), no. 10, http://www.vatican.va/content/john-paul-ii/en/letters/1979/documents/hf_jp-ii_let_19790409_sacerdoti-giovedi-santo.html.

4. Pope John Paul II, "General Audience" (March 31, 1993), http://www.vatican.va/content/john-paul-ii/fr/audiences/1993/documents/hf_jp-ii_aud_19930331.html.

5. Pope John Paul II, "Homily at Mass for the Conclusion of the World Retreat for Priests" (October 9, 1984), no. 2, http://www.vatican.va/content/john-paul-ii/it/homilies/1984/documents/hf_jp-ii_hom_19841009_sacerdoti.html.

6. Pope John Paul II, "Homily at Mass for the Conclusion of the World Retreat for Priests" (September 18, 1990), no. 6, https://w2.vatican.va/content/john-paul-ii/it/homilies/1990/documents/hf_jp-ii_hom_19900918_ritiro-sacedoti.html.

7. Pope John Paul II, "Discorso al clero italiano" (February 16, 1984), no. 3.

8. Pope John Paul II, post-synodal apostolic exhortation *Reconciliatio et Paenitentia* (December 2, 1984), no. 23, http://www.vatican.va/content/john-paul-ii/en/apost_exhortations/documents/hf_jp-ii_exh_02121984_reconciliatio-et-paenitentia.html.

9. Pope John Paul II, *Letter to Priests on the Occasion of Holy Thursday 1979*, no. 11.

10. Pope John Paul II, "General Audience" (June 30, 1993), no. 5, http://www.vatican.va/content/john-paul-ii/fr/audiences/1993/documents/hf_jp-ii_aud_19930630.html.

11. Pope John Paul II, "General Audience," no. 5.

12. Pope John Paul II, *Letter to Priests on the Occasion of Holy Thursday 1979*, no. 11.

13. Pope Benedict XVI, "Letter Proclaiming a Year for Priests" (June 16, 2009), http://w2.vatican.va/content/benedict-xvi/en/letters/2009/documents/hf_ben-xvi_let_20090616_anno-sacerdotale.html.

14. Pope Benedict XVI, "Address to Members of the Congregation of the Clergy" (March 16, 2009), http://www.vatican.va/content/benedict-xvi/en/speeches/2009/march/documents/hf_ben-xvi_spe_20090316_plenaria-clero.html.

15. Pope Benedict XVI, "Chrism Mass Homily" (April 9, 2009), http://w2.vatican.va/content/benedict-xvi/en/homilies/2009/documents/hf_ben-xvi_hom_20090409_messa-crismale.html.

16. Pope Benedict XVI, "Chrism Mass Homily."

17. Pope Benedict XVI, post-synodal apostolic exhortation *Sacramentum Caritatis* (February 22, 2007), no. 23, http://www.vatican.va/content/benedict-xvi/en/apost_exhortations/documents/hf_ben-xvi_exh_20070222_sacramentum-caritatis.html.

18. Joseph Ratzinger with Vittorio Messori, *The Ratzinger Report: An Exclusive Interview on the State of the Church*, trans. Salvator Attanasio and Graham Harrison (San Francisco: Ignatius Press, 1985), 126.

19. Ratzinger, *The Ratzinger Report*, 126.

20. Pope Benedict XVI, "Meeting with Priests of the Diocese of Albano" (August 31, 2006), http://w2.vatican.va/content/benedict-xvi/en/speeches/2006/august/documents/hf_ben-xvi_spe_20060831_sacerdoti-albano.html.

21. Pope Benedict XVI, "Homily for Mass for the Ordination to Priesthood of 19 Deacons of the Diocese of Rome" (May 3, 2009), http://www.vatican.va/content/benedict-xvi/en/homilies/2009/documents/hf_ben-xvi_hom_20090503_ordinazioni-sacerdotali.html.

22. Pope Benedict XVI, "Meeting with the Parish Priests of the Diocese of Rome" (February 18, 2010), http://w2.vatican.va/content/benedict-xvi/en/speeches/2010/february/documents/hf_ben-xvi_spe_20100218_parroci-roma.html.

23. Pope Benedict XVI, "Homily, Eucharist with Seminarians, Apostolic Journey to Madrid on the Occasion of the 26th World Youth Day" (August 20, 2011), http://www.vatican.va/content/benedict-xvi/en/homilies/2011/documents/hf_ben-xvi_hom_20110820_seminaristi-madrid.html.

24. Pope Benedict XVI, "Homily for Mass for the Beginning of the Petrine Ministry of the Bishop of Rome" (April 24, 2005), http://www.vatican.va/content/benedict-xvi/en/homilies/2005/documents/hf_ben-xvi_hom_20050424_inizio-pontificato.html.

25. Pope Francis, "Homily for Holy Chrism Mass" (April 17, 2014), http://w2.vatican.va/content/francesco/en/homilies/2014/documents/papa-francesco_20140417_omelia-crisma.html.

26. Pope Francis, "Homily for Holy Chrism Mass."

27. Pope Francis, "Homily for Holy Chrism Mass."

28. Pope Francis, "Homily for Holy Chrism Mass."

29. Pope Francis, "Homily for Holy Chrism Mass."

30. Pope Francis, "Homily for Holy Chrism Mass."

31. Pope Francis, "Address to Rectors and Students of the Pontifical Colleges and Residences of Rome" (May 12, 2014), http://www.vatican.va/content/francesco/en/speeches/2014/may/documents/papa-francesco_20140512_pontifici-collegi-convitti.html.

32. Pope Francis, "Address to Rectors and Students."

33. Pope Francis, "Address to Rectors and Students."

34. Pope Francis, "Address to Participants in the 37th National Convocation of the Renewal in the Holy Spirit" (June 1, 2014), http://www.vatican.va/content/francesco/en/speeches/2014/june/documents/papa-francesco_20140601_rinnovamento-spirito-santo.html.

35. Pope Francis, "Address to the Plenary of the Congregation for the Clergy" (October 3, 2014), http://w2.vatican.va/content/francesco/en/speeches/2014/october/documents/papa-francesco_20141003_plenaria-congregazione-clero.html.

36. Pope Francis with Antonio Spadaro, *My Door Is Always Open: A Conversation on Faith, Hope and the Church in A Time of Change*, trans. Shaun Whiteside (London: Bloomsbury, 2013), 131.

37. Pope Francis, "Address to Participants in the Convention on the 50th Anniversary of the Conciliar Decrees *Optatam Totius* and *Presbyterorum Ordinis*" (November 20, 2015), https://w2.vatican.va/content/francesco/en/speeches/2015/november/documents/papa-francesco_20151120_formazione-sacerdoti.html.

38. Pope Francis, "Morning Meditation in the Chapel of the *Domus Sanctae Marthae*" (November 10, 2014), http://www.vatican.va/content/francesco/en/cotidie/2014/documents/papa-francesco-cotidie_20141110_sinful-christians.html.

39. Pope Francis, "Morning Meditation in the Chapel of the *Domus Sanctae Marthae*" (January 27, 2014), http://www

.vatican.va/content/francesco/en/cotidie/2014/documents/papa-francesco-cotidie_20140127_priests-news.html.

40. Pope Francis, "Morning Meditation in the Chapel of the *Domus Sanctae Marthae*" (January 27, 2014).

41. Pope Francis, "Morning Meditation in the Chapel of the *Domus Sanctae Marthae*" (January 11, 2014), http://www.vatican.va/content/francesco/en/cotidie/2014/documents/papa-francesco-cotidie_20140111_priest.html.

42. Pope Francis, "Address to the Italian Episcopal Conference" (May 16, 2016), no. 1, http://www.vatican.va/content/francesco/en/speeches/2016/may/documents/papa-francesco_20160516_cei.html.

43. Pope Francis, "Homily for Mass with Priestly Ordinations" (May 11, 2014), http://www.vatican.va/content/francesco/en/homilies/2014/documents/papa-francesco_20140511_omelia-ordinazioni-presbiterali.html.

44. Pope Francis, "Homily, Third Worldwide Priests' Retreat" (June 12, 2015), http://www.vatican.va/content/francesco/en/homilies/2015/documents/papa-francesco_20150612_omelia-ritiro-mondiale-sacerdoti.html.

45. Pope Francis, "Address to the Missionaries of Mercy" (February 9, 2016), http://www.vatican.va/content/francesco/en/speeches/2016/february/documents/papa-francesco_20160209_missionari-misericordia.html.

46. Pope Francis, "Address to Rectors and Students."